The Wicker Park Kid

Sherwin J. Ernst

Cover design by Scott Gaunt: scottgaunt@hotmail.co.uk

ISBN: 978-1-71684-461-4

PublishNation LLC
www.publishnation.net

This book is dedicated to my Wicker Park family, to my wife Sandra, and to my children: Matthew, Lynda and Jon.

A Note About Wicker Park

Chicago's Wicker Park neighborhood, on the Near Northwest Side, has a rich and colorful history. It is a special place not only to me but to the many thousands of others who have lived in it over the years.

The area was settled in 1871, after the Chicago Fire, by prosperous Scandinavian and German beer and wine merchants who found they weren't welcome on Prairie Avenue, home to the city's old-guard elite. Undaunted, the immigrants created an elegant enclave of extravagant Victorian mansions around the tiny 4.3-acre triangular park that bears the family name of the brothers who had donated the land to the city. While the mansions were clustered on certain streets, cottages, two-flats and row houses were soon built nearby to house servants and office workers.

After the turn of the century, thousands of Polish, Jewish and other European immigrants moved into the neighborhood, eventually turning it into a diverse mix of ethnic backgrounds and social classes, with lower-middle, middle and upper classes living in close proximity. This is the Wicker Park I remember.

Wicker Park fell on hard times as a result of the housing shortage after World War II. Many of the beautiful Victorians were divided into rooming houses. By the 1960s, slumlords, arson, gangs, and graffiti-covered walls characterized the once pleasant neighborhood.

Fortunately, that isn't the end of the Wicker Park story. Many of the mansions survived, and by the mid-seventies young professionals had begun to move in and rehabilitate and revitalize the area. Today, many of the homes have been restored to their former splendor, new housing has been built, and Wicker Park is once again a desirable neighborhood, whose residents are working together to create and maintain a very special community in this one-square-mile oasis.

Our knowledge is from our own firsthand experience,
not from books or hearsay.

Sant Rajinder Singh Ji Maharaj

Chapter 1

It was October, 1961, near Chicago's City Hall. It was what you might call a small wedding-Sandy, myself and Elmer Tone, justice of the peace.

After the ceremony, we stood outside for a minute, across from City Hall, before starting to walk back toward my office on LaSalle Street, Chicago's financial district.

I owned a small insurance agency, and Sandy was my secretary, Gal Friday and Fun Time companion.

We had met a year earlier at a cocktail party and hit it off. I had just started my own business on a shoestring and had managed to get her to come to work for me, first part-time and then eventually full-time.

My staff consisted of an office manager, Marshall, whom I had known since I was about eleven, Sandy, her assistant, and a couple of salespeople. At that point in my career, I was still out selling full-time, as the office was kept well under control between Sandy and Marshall.

As Sandy looked at the bright yellow color around her ring finger, I said, "Don't call your mother until after five o'clock, and don't mention this to anybody at the office before five."

I kissed her on the cheek and left to get my car and go out selling.

Although I was born in Chicago in 1932, my parents lost everything in the ensuing depression years, and we moved to Louisville, Kentucky, when I was six.

I can still remember Chicago's Wicker Park area and our third-floor apartment. We all lived together-my father, mother, aunt, two uncles, my two cousins and me.

I attended kindergarten in Wicker Park, I had my tonsils and adenoids removed when we lived in Wicker Park, I took the streetcar from Wicker Park with my mother when she went shopping in downtown Chicago. I was always fascinated by the full-sized stuffed white horse in one of the shop windows we passed as we rode the streetcar. I enjoyed thundering through the tunnel under the Chicago River, and I used to wish the tunnel was longer as the rays of light reappeared and we approached downtown.

I remember the alley behind our Wicker Park apartment. I was always excited when my father arrived with his horse and wagon. I thought my dad's having a horse was neat. His having to struggle to earn a living selling fruits and vegetables from his wagon was normal for me. I wasn't ashamed, I was proud-my father had a horse!

What a difference a few years can make. When I was born, my father owned several fruit stands, property, and a car. My mother had a housekeeper. They had been grieving over the death of their daughter, Fay. She had died four years earlier of meningitis; she was just seven years old. I was the only child. My two cousins, Deanie and Shirley, were like daughters to my mother and father. Deanie was the same age as my sister Fay; they used to dress alike, they looked alike. My cousin Shirley was three years older than I. We fought a lot. Shirley and Deanie had a sister, the middle child. She died the same week my sister died. My cousins were like my sisters and I was like their baby brother. Their mother was not like my aunt; she was like my second mother. My cousin's father was not like an uncle; he was part of my family. My mother's and aunt's bachelor brother lived with us. He was more than an uncle; he was part of us.

2

My father had already left for Louisville. He had decided on Louisville because he had a brother in the grocery business there. Things were not great in Louisville, but anything seemed better than Chicago at that time. If my father hadn't had a brother in Louisville, chances are he would have gone to Los Angeles. He'd heard talk that opportunities seemed good in Los Angeles, but Louisville seemed safer. After all, it was just 300 miles from Chicago, instead of more than 2,000, and besides, he had family there.

It was the summer of 1938, and my father had sent for my mother and me. He had a job working in the wholesale fruit and vegetable business. He found us an apartment at Preston and Walnut streets, above a five-and-ten-cent store, five blocks from the Haymarket, the city's combination wholesale produce market and retail farmer's market.

I was excited-it was my first train ride. My father met us with big hugs at Louisville's Union Station. I met an uncle, aunt, and two cousins there, for the first time. We all went to the apartment. It wasn't the same. I missed everyone in Chicago. That night I cried myself to sleep.

As the years passed, things turned better financially for my father. He had his own wholesale fruit and vegetable business. My mother and I would go to Chicago by train every Christmas and summer school vacation. We stayed with my aunt, uncles, Shirley and Deanie at their new apartment on Chicago's Northwest Side, on Lyndale Street. I became friendly with the kids on the block and I was known as "Kentuck". One of those kids was Marshall, who, years later, would be my comptroller.

We had moved from Preston and Walnut. My parents bought a house in the Highlands section of Louisville. My dad bought me a 1947 Chevrolet when I was seventeen.

A year later, I joined the Air Force. After basic training at Lackland Air Force Base in Texas, I was stationed at Sheppard AFB in Wichita Falls, Texas, before going to McCord AFB in

Tacoma, Washington. After that it was on to Frankfurt, Germany, and then to Paris for my final two years.

I returned to Louisville and went to work for my father. That lasted for about two years before I decided to move to Chicago and find a job there. Looking back, I realize that Louisville was really a great place to grow up. But I missed Chicago.

My father was fourteen when he arrived in America, alone. He came from Eastern Europe, from a province in Poland called Galicia, where he had lived with his family -his parents and his younger brothers and sisters- in a farming area near the trading town of Lemberg. His father was a kind of broker, selling cattle and horses; even the nobility of Poland and Austria would buy his animals. He was not a rich man, however, and life was always a struggle. From the small framed picture of my dad's parents that rested on a table in our living room I could tell that my grandfather was a very pious Jew. In the picture he has a long beard and wears a hat; the coat over his suit almost touches the ground.

In Chicago my father learned English and taught himself to read and write. Later, he brought over his three brothers and one sister; his parents and two other sisters stayed behind, and years later, perished in the Holocaust.

My grandfather and grandmother on my mother's side came to America from Lithuania, bringing their three children. My mother was the youngest; she was nine when they arrived. Although my mother's parents had died in Chicago before I was born, I knew them from the photo portraits hanging on the living room wall. My mother's father was an Orthodox rabbi; the Hebrew Theological College in Skokie, Illinois, has the originals of the books he wrote. In the picture he wears an elevated square yarmulke and has a beard. He looks very religious and strict.

Between my mother's and father's families, I had an awful lot of aunts, uncles and first cousins living in Chicago. I always had the feeling that I was the favorite-I belonged in Chicago.

After Sandy and I started dating, I would tell her about my family. I told her about my sister, Fay, who died before I was born. I told her about how inseparable my mother and her sister were. I told her about how I thought I was not my mother's child. I reasoned that my mother couldn't have any more children, and my aunt, who was my real mother, gave me to her sister. I told her about the time I was stationed in Washington and one day, while in Seattle, I looked for my mother's name in the phone book; I had this strange feeling that my real mother was living in Seattle. But that didn't make sense, for if I reasoned that my aunt was my mother, why would I have this feeling that my real mother was in Seattle? And why would I look her up under my mother's name? It was nice to have someone to talk to, someone who didn't care if you were crazy.

My parents had moved back to Chicago a few years before I met Sandy. They had a small apartment on the North Side. I always stopped by to see them once a week, and I took them to various family get-togethers. Between Bar Mitzvahs, weddings and funerals, I saw everyone a couple of times a year. My Wicker Park family, I usually saw at least twice a month.

Because my mother had been brought up in an Orthodox Jewish home, tradition was very important to her. So, when I told her I was bringing this girl, Sandy, from Denver, who worked for me, over for dinner on one of the Jewish holidays, she was pleasantly surprised. Of all the women in the family, my mother's cooking was the best-everyone all said so, and it was true. My mother didn't ask me what she probably wanted to: "Is she Jewish?" (During the dinner she was overjoyed to discover that in fact, Sandy was Jewish.) She was probably remembering the time when I lived in Paris and was engaged to a French girl named Piou-short for Pierrette. She was probably remembering the time in Louisville when I was a teenager and two of my friends carried me to my door around two o'clock in the morning, rang the bell and drove off, leaving me leaning against the door in my drunken stupor.

I was different from all the other cousins in the family. I belonged, but yet I didn't belong. There were times as a youngster when I felt embarrassed about my Jewishness, especially when my parents would speak Yiddish in public places where gentiles could hear. And when I grew older, I saw nothing wrong in marrying outside of my faith if I found the right girl. I knew my mother and father would be hurt, but I didn't care. I never bragged about my female conquests as so many other guys did. To me it was all very private and kind of sacred, too.

A month after Sandy and I got married by the justice of the peace, we got married by a rabbi. The only people attending the small ceremony in his study were my Wicker Park family, Deanie's and Shirley's husbands, Marty and Sydney, and my in-laws and Sandy's two younger brothers.

Afterward, we had all the family and friends over to our coach house on Burton Place, in the Old Town section. The coach house was two stories high and everything was marble and tile: the floors, the walls, the stairs and railing to the second-floor bedrooms. I had rented it just before we decided to get married. It was the perfect bachelor's pad, with its fireplace and thirty-foot-high ceiling. It was expensive, though, and the heating bills were a killer.

A few weeks later, my father's brother and his wife had us over to their home in suburban Lincolnwood. My parents and all the aunts, uncles and cousins were there. It was a lovely evening, and Sandy was accepted as part of this huge, warm family. I had left to get the car after saying my good-byes, planning to have Sandy meet me out front about ten minutes later. By that time, the heater would have warmed the car.

We rode in silence while I paid close attention to the snowy streets. The silence was broken when she said, "Sherwin, what would you do if you knew something about me, and you knew if you told me about it, it might hurt me? Would you tell me?"

She really got me curious. I said, "I don't know. Why?"

"Well, I just wanted to know."

I sensed something very strange in the serious tone of her question. I slowly turned my head to look at her. A surge of inner knowledge swept my being as our eyes met. "I'm adopted, aren't I?" I asked softly, smiling.

"Yes." Sandy was amazed by my reaction and seemed relieved at my calmness. The feelings I'd had all these years-I was right! I was deeply relieved by her confirmation.

"How did you find out?" I asked.

"I've known for over a week."

"What! You've known for over a week? Why didn't you tell me?" I was starting to get irritated. "Who told you?"

"Your cousin Melvin."

Melvin is a third cousin on my mother's side of the family, an attorney with offices in my LaSalle Street building. "Melvin. How did he know?"

"Melvin always knew."

"Why did he tell you?"

"Because, now that we're married, he felt I should know in case there might be some type of inheritance from your natural parents."

"Who are my parents?"

"I don't know, and Melvin doesn't know. I don't know who does know."

"Why did you wait until now to tell me?" I asked.

"Tonight, when you went to get the car, your Aunt Dora was kissing me and welcoming me into the family. Everyone was there, and Aunt Dora jokingly said, 'You and Sherwin look so much alike, who knows? Maybe you're brother and sis...' She slapped her hand over her mouth and then said something in Yiddish. Your mother almost fell backward, and I knew if you had been there, you would have picked up on what she meant, and that would be an awful way for you to find out."

"I don't want my folks to know that I know," I said. "My God! If Melvin knows, that means that Shirley and Deanie must know." I thought for a moment and then said, "I don't want anyone to know that I know."

When we arrived home, we went to bed. We left the lights on...we talked about how I could find out...if I was adopted, there had to be adoption papers. Tomorrow, I would go to City Hall and find out what I could.

The following morning I walked to City Hall from my office. At the Adoption Bureau I told the woman behind the counter that I wanted to check out some adoption papers. Since I was wearing a suit, she must have assumed I was an attorney. She directed me to the clerk of the adoption court.

I found the courtroom. The day's proceedings hadn't yet started, and the judge's chair was empty. The room was crowded with couples, infants and young children. I saw a man shuffling papers next to the judge's bench. I approached and asked if he was the clerk of the court. He was. I introduced myself, explained that I had recently discovered I was adopted, and asked for his help in locating my natural parents. He hesitated. I remained silent, waiting for him to speak. He seemed to be studying me.

"Have a seat, and when this court session is over, we'll talk," he finally said.

I thanked him and took a seat toward the rear of the courtroom. I looked at all the couples with their infants. They seemed tense, but happy. I thought of how I must have been here twenty-nine years ago, with my mother and father.

The judge entered, everyone stood, court was called to order. The couples with their infants and children each had their turn before the judge. The atmosphere was friendly and joyful; the judge was kind. One after another, he finalized adoption papers. The tension dissipated, and everyone was aglow. Finally, the session was ended, and the clerk motioned me forward. "I'll be through in a few minutes. Then we can go back by my office and talk."

We walked back to the Adoption Bureau, where I repeated that I wanted to find my natural parents. He asked my name again, my adoptive parents' name, my date of birth. He wrote down the information. "Wait here a moment," he said. He walked through a doorway, and I could see row after row of legal-size file cabinets. It seemed like an eternity before he returned, papers in hand. "Follow me to my office," he said.

It was a small room, and I sat across from his desk. "I cannot let you have these," he said, "but go ahead and write the information down." He handed me paper and pencil.

There it was. My parents' names and two other names-Abe Safran and Sarah Safran- and then another name, the name of a three-month-old boy-Nathaniel Safran. That was me. Nathaniel Safran. There was other information: dates and a description of the petition and decree. I copied all the details.

"That's all I have to show you. I have no other information."

I shook his hand warmly. "Thank you so much," I said. He smiled, and I hurried back to my office.

I couldn't wait to share the information with Sandy. She came into my private office and closed the door. "My real name is Nathaniel Safran," I explained. "My natural parents are Abe and Sarah Safran...get me a phone book...let's start there!"

Nothing. There were no Safrans. A city the size of Chicago, and nobody named Safran. I tried all the suburbs; still no Safran. We went back to the coach house. I called Information in several other cities. Detroit had a Safran; I called. They had never heard of an Abe or Sarah Safran. "This is silly," I said. "I have to think this through. I must be overlooking something."

9

Sandy and I were lying in bed. She was reading. I was thinking. "Wow!" I had it! "Nathaniel Safran must have been born in Chicago...that means there has to be a birth certificate. Tomorrow I'm going to the place where they have the birth certificates and ask for a copy of it!" Sandy put her book down. She was excited for me.

The next morning, I found the Bureau of Vital Statistics just a few blocks from my office. An elevated train roared along the tracks above Wells Street. The sound made me quicken my pace.

I got off the elevator and went to the counter. "I would like a copy of my birth certificate," I said to the clerk. She gave me an application to fill out.

Name...I wrote *Nathaniel Safran*. Date of birth ... *February 22, 1932*. Place of birth...*Chicago* (I hoped.)

Name of father ...*Abe Safran*

Maiden name of mother ...just wrote *Sarah*.

I handed the application to the clerk. She returned shortly. "That will be one dollar."

There were quite a few people in the room. Some were waiting; others were filling out papers. The Bureau had records for marriages, births, deaths and perhaps more, I didn't know. I had needed my birth certificate twice before-in Louisville, when I first applied for my driver's license, and when I enlisted in the Air Force. I still had a mental image of that legal document with a seal that read "'State of Illinois, County of Cook, Certification of Birth" and my name and date of birth.

I went to the side of the room, sat on a chair, and started to read my new-found treasure. The moment of truth had arrived. I gulped as I read the heading in the top right corner: Original Certificate of Birth. Unlike my regular certification of birth, the only one I'd ever seen before, this document was full of information. I felt almost hypnotized by this paper of facts. A quick glance showed different names, addresses, occupations

10

and numbers. I started to read slowly from the top. The chill of the unknown crept through my body. I was about to discover myself.

Full name of child: *Nathaniel Safran*

Sex of child: *M*

Full Term: *Y*

Date of Birth: *2/22/32*

Father: *Safran, Abe*

Residence: *2849 W.Division* "I'll have to check that out," I thought

Color or Race: *White*

Age last birthday: *33* "He was four years older than I am now."

Birthplace: *Poland* "That's interesting;"

Occupation: *Tailor*

Date, month and year last employed: *Unemployed June, 1931* "Well, apparently there was a money problem."

Mother: *Green, Sarah* I read it again. I tried to think whether I knew anyone named Green. I didn't.

Residence: *2849 W. Division* "Same as Abe."

Age last birthday: *24* "Wow! Same age as Sandy."

Birthplace: *Poland* "I wonder if they got married there?"

Occupation: *Housewife* "Well, nobody was working."

I put the birth certificate down, the print was small and everything else looked so legal. I paused for a moment, and my eyes went immediately to *Mother, Sarah, Age, 24.* "Wow, I wonder what she looked like. I bet she was beautiful. Let's see...she would be fifty-three now. I wonder if she's alive. I'm going to find her, and if she's dead, I'll find her grave." I sighed, I rubbed my eyes. I was fighting back a flood of emotions as I went back to the fine print.

"Uh, that's interesting. I missed it...I was born at Michael Reese Hospital. Oh, there's something else...born alive 11:05 p.m. I wonder what else I missed. Let me go through this again." I restudied the details about Abe; I tried to imagine what he must have looked like. I couldn't. "Let's see, he was thirty-three...shit, he'd be sixty-two now. He was nine years older than Sarah."

I continued reading in silence.

Treatment given child's eyes at birth: *Crede*. "Whatever the hell that is."

Doctor: *H.J. Smith*. "Maybe I can find him."

Line 27...Number of children of this mother (at moment of this birth and including this child) (a) Born alive and now living: *2* ..."Holy shit!" My adrenaline going, I got up and went back to the counter. I waited impatiently to catch the attention of a clerk.

Finally. "Yes, can I help you?"

"I sure hope so." I told her that I had just discovered I was adopted, and I gave her my name and showed her the birth certificate. "This says my real name is Nathaniel Safran. See here," I said, pointing to line 27, "I have a brother or sister. They must have a birth certificate here...can you help me?"

"Yes, I see." She called a supervisor over and repeated my story to her. Soon I had four clerks clustered around, all interested in trying to help me. "Wait here," the second one said. She disappeared in the rear behind rows of files.

It must have been twenty minutes, although it seemed longer. She returned my certificate to me. She was holding another birth certificate. "Here," she said, placing the certificate on the counter so we could both read it. "You have a sister," she said. "Sylvia Safran," I read, "Hey! Look at this...She was born on February 22nd, the same day I was born! Let's see, 1927. She's five years older than me." A couple of the other clerks heard my voice and came over...they looked at both certificates with interest "Do you have any suggestions on how I can find her?" I asked the supervisor.

"Maybe she's married," she replied. "So, how could I find that out?"

"Let me check the marriage licenses. We have them right here." She took my sister's certificate. "I'll be back in a little while," she said.

I waited and waited. She returned. There was a look of disappointment on her face. "I'm sorry, I couldn't find anything."

"Thanks very, very much. That was really nice of you. Good-bye." I nodded goodbye to the other clerks.

"Good luck," they called.

I left with both certificates in my hand. Back to the coach house, the tiled kitchen counter, the phone. Forget the office. I had important business to attend to. I needed to think. "Damn it, there's got to be a way," I thought. The phone rang.

"Hi, Hon. How's it going?" Sandy asked.

I told her the story. "Wow," she said.

"Yeah," I answered.

"Marshall asked where you were. He needs some papers signed. I told him you weren't feeling good. I'll bring them home tonight."

"OK," I agreed.

Sandy came home at about six. I handed her the birth certificates. She read them. "I've been studying them all afternoon. Here, let me show you something." I laid them side by side and put my finger on the certificate of Nathaniel Safran where it said "residence." "They were living at 2849 West Division Street. Now, look at my sister's certificate. See here." I pointed. "When my sister was born, they were living at 916 North Kedzie. Division Street is all Puerto Rican now, and Kedzie is all black. So, what I'm going to do tomorrow is go down to City Hall and look up old voter registrations. If I track down some of their old neighbors, maybe someone will remember them."

"That's a good idea, Sherwin," Sandy said.

"Here, let me show you something else. See here, on my birth certificate, where it shows occupation?"

"Yes."

"Well, look, Abe was unemployed. Now look at my sister's...See? He was employed as a tailor. Now, look at mine...See? Number of children now living, two."

"Yes."

"That's how I found out I had a sister!"

"Yeah, I didn't pick that up," Sandy said.

"Don't feel bad. I've been looking at these all afternoon!"

The next morning, I was at City Hall. I located the room that had the old voter registration records. A clerk approached me.

"I'd like to see the names of the people who were registered to vote at 2849 West Division in 1932," I said. He wrote down the address and year and disappeared behind high shelves at the end of the counter. I moved toward the end, so I could follow his movements. He climbed a ladder; everything seemed organized ...old, dirty, dusty...but orderly. He climbed down, carrying three large ledger books. He blew off the dust, wiped them clean, and placed them in front of me on the counter. "Here, look through these."

It was as if I was in a time gone by. I turned the pages slowly, until I found 2849 West Division Street. I copied the few names I found. I copied names from across the street, names from either side of 2849. I saw no Safrans. I had copied twelve names. "That's a start," I thought.

I returned to the coach house, the tile counter, the phone book, the phone. I realized that finding someone from twenty-nine years ago who lived on the 2800 block of Division Street would be difficult, let alone finding someone who knew an Abe or Sarah Safran. But, what the hell....I went to work. It was still early in the day. I got a lot of no answers; the few people I did speak to had never heard of Abe or Sarah Safran. I called later in the evening-same results. Never heard of them. I tried Information for suburban listings, no luck. Sandy came home at around eight. We talked, I called more numbers. It was a dead end.

The following days, I followed up on previous ideas. Doctors, hospitals, missing persons bureaus...nothing gave any hope. I thought, "What if they're dead?" I wanted to be able to see the graves. I had to know, I had to know who I was, who they were. I knew I couldn't rest until I found out.

One night, while Sandy slept, I lay in bed on my back. My thoughts were on the birth certificates. I had read and studied them so much, I could visualize every line. I knew there were avenues I hadn't covered, but what? All the calls to people from twenty nine years ago....I knew that wasn't the answer...but what?

"Oh, my God," I murmured. "That's it!" I jumped out of bed and ran downstairs to the kitchen counter. I put both certificates together. "That's it!"

I ran upstairs.

"Sandy, wake up, wake up!" I urged. She sat up groggily.

"Look," I said, putting both certificates in front of her. "What?"

"Look," I repeated. "Nathaniel Safran; Occupation of father-unemployed."

"So?"

"Look now," I said. "Sylvia Safran; Occupation of father-tailor."

"But we saw that."

"Don't you get it?" She didn't.

"Occupation, tailor. That means he must have belonged to a union!"

"You know, you might be right. So what are you going to do?"

15

"I know I'm right! Tomorrow, tomorrow, I'm going to check out the unions!"

The next morning, I was up early. I'd had a good three or four hours sleep....was awake, fresh and ready to go. Coffee at hand, cigarettes in hand, phone by my side. The kitchen counter was my desk. I was at work.

Sandy had left for work. At 8:30, I dialed Information. "I'd like the phone number of the Tailors Union."

"I'm sorry, we have no listing like that"

"Well, just give me the phone number of any union."

I called the Teamsters Union and asked what union tailors would belong to. I was given the number for the Amalgamated Clothing Textile Workers Union. I dialed.

"I'm trying to locate someone who was a tailor and probably belonged to your union," I began. I was transferred to the records department.

"Let me check it out How do you spell Safran?" the man asked. I spelled it for him. "Just a moment," he said.

He came back on the phone after about five minutes of silence. "We had an Abe Safran up to 1954," he reported.

"Do you know where he is now?"

"Nope. The last place we show him working is the Wilson Shop on Franklin Street"

"Thank you," I said.

"Information, may I help you?" the operator asked.

"The phone number of the Wilson Shop."

I dialed and asked for Personnel. Abe Safran did not work there.

I double-checked the address and drove there. It was about seven blocks from my office. I went to the Personnel Department and asked to speak to the manager. I introduced myself, told him I had recently discovered I was adopted, and had found out that my father had worked for his company. I asked for his help.

16

He invited me into his office. "Have a seat. Let me check out his file," he offered. "Yeah, he worked here. Left in 1954. I wasn't here then."

"Would there be anyone here who might have known him?"

"There's an old-timer that still works here. Wait here, let me go down in the shop and ask." He seemed genuinely interested in getting answers for me.

After a while, he returned. "You're in luck! A close friend of Abe's still works here.

He wasn't known as Abe around here, though."

"Not known as Abe?"

"No. He was called The Professor." I smiled.

"The Professor," I thought.

He directed me to the shop a few floors below and told me to ask for Mr. Olshinsky. "Thanks very much, I appreciate it," I said, as he nodded good-bye. I took the elevator down, where the door opened onto the shop floor. Men and women, all working in this large open space. Everyone seemed to be working on patterns with their sewing machines; it was noisy, but not deafening.

"May I help you?" a man asked.

"Yes, I was told to see Mr. Olshinsky."

"Back there," he pointed. I walked to the rear.

"Are you Mr. Olshinsky?" I asked.

"Yes."

"The personnel manager said you know Abe Safran."

"The Professor...everyone knew The Professor. What is it you want?" He looked at me curiously.

"I have some personal business with him, and I'd like to contact him. Do you know where he is?"

"Yeah, but he's not in Chicago. We have written each other. Why do you want to know? Who are you?"

I explained the true story of how I had just learned that Abe Safran was my natural father. He hesitated; I could feel his caution, and he must have felt my plea.

"Tell you what, why don't you come over to my house tonight. I want to talk to my wife....I never knew he had a son, he never mentioned a son. I know he has a daughter. I just want to be sure. You come over the house around seven."

"Can I bring my wife?"

"Oh, sure." He gave me his address and we shook hands good-bye. I drove back to my office and hurriedly took the elevator to my floor. I couldn't wait to share everything with Sandy.

"Sherwin! Where have you been?" Marshall asked. He was on the phone, his hand covering the mouthpiece.

"I'll tell you later. Tell Sandy to come into my office when she gets off the phone." I turned to Sandy's assistant, "Hold any calls for me." Everyone was on the phone, the office was busy, my desk was clear. "Good old Sandy," I thought. She brought me a cup of coffee and closed my door.

"Well?" she asked.

"I found Abe."

"Where? How?"

I went through the whole story, all the details. "They used to call him 'The Professor'," I finished. "This Mr. Olshinsky seemed reluctant about giving me Abe's address. I want to be there at seven sharp."

Sandy and I drove to Chicago's North Side. We stood in the hallway for a few minutes. I looked at my watch, and at seven sharp, I rang the bell.

It was a three-flat. They lived on the first floor. They greeted us cordially, and then Mrs. Olshinsky offered us coffee. The four of us sat in their living room and chatted. I requested Abe's address.

"Maybe I should write and let him know you're looking for him." Mr. Olshinsky was hesitant.

"Well, I'd like to get his address and write to him myself," I said quietly.

The Olshinskys looked at each other. Mr. Olshinsky left the room. He returned with an address book. "Here," he said, showing me the book. "He lives in California Canoga Park, California."

"Where's Canoga Park?"

"I think it's near Los Angeles," he replied.

I wrote down the address. "Thank you very much," I said as we left.

Sandy and I returned to the coach house, and I sat at the kitchen counter and wrote:

> *"Dear Abe:*
>
> *I recently discovered that I was adopted.*
>
> *Locating you was not an easy task; it took a lot of time, determination, research and leg work. I hold no animosity towards you or Sarah but I am overwhelmed with curiosity as to why and what circumstances led to your decision to give away a baby boy.*
>
> *You could not have possibly picked two more sincere and warm people than the parents I now have. They are not aware of the fact that I know of the adoption and keeping this knowledge from them is extremely important to me.*
>
> *I would like very much to meet you at some future time.*
>
> *You may write in care of Sandra Levitt, 160 West Burton Place, Chicago, Ill.*
>
> *Hoping to hear from you, Nathaniel*

I handed the letter to Sandy and asked her to type it on our portable typewriter. "Why 'in care of Sandra Levitt'?" Sandy was puzzled.

"I just don't want him to know my name right now."

Sandy typed the letter. She changed "Dear Abe" to "Dear Mr. Safran." "Why did you do that?"

"It seems more respectful," she responded.

I was upset. I felt more comfortable using "Dear Abe," but I didn't make an issue of it. I signed the letter Nathaniel. It was a strange feeling writing my birth name.

I mailed the letter early the next morning, slowly dropping it into the mailbox. I hoped for a reply in two to three weeks. I had done all I could. I went out selling...It had been an exhausting ten days.

Chapter 2

Everything was back to normal. Sandy and I went to my folks' house for lunch that Sunday. I was very protective of my parents, of keeping them from finding out that I knew- the same as they had been all these years of not telling me I was adopted. I was thinking about all the times, as a kid growing up in Louisville, when I sassed back my mother. I was thinking of when I was a kid, and if I had known, how I probably would have said, "I don't have to listen to you! You're not my real mother!" There was no question in my mind that, in my particular case, they had done the right thing by not telling me I was adopted. I was their son; nothing had changed.

It was one evening the following week, when Sandy and I had returned home from the office. Sandy removed the mail from our mailbox. "Sherwin, you have a special delivery letter from California," she exclaimed. She handed me the envelope.

I looked at all the four-cent Lincoln and one-cent Washington stamps. It was addressed to Nathaniel, c/o Sandra Levitt. There was a return address in Canoga Park...no name. A special delivery stamp. It looked so official. I slowly opened the envelope and began to read the letter aloud to Sandy.

"Dearest Nathaniel, Your letter was like a miracle! You have no idea how many times I have thought about you, nor longed to know of your whereabouts. I was barely five..." "*Holy shit, it's from my sister,*" I breathed. I continued reading:

"I was barely five when you were born, but I remember very well the little brother who was taken from me all too soon. At first, I was told that you had died of a cold.

21

Later, as I grew old enough to understand, I learned of your having been given away for adoption.

"Let me assure you that you were loved and wanted ..."

I started to get choked up. I looked at Sandy. "Let's sit down, and you read it."

Sandy read the letter aloud, starting from the beginning.

Nov. 24, 1961

Dearest Nathaniel,

Your letter was like a miracle! You have no idea how many times I have thought about you, nor longed to know of your whereabouts. I was barely five when you were born, but I remember very well the little brother who was taken from me all too soon. At first, I was told that you had died of a cold. Later, as I grew old enough to understand I learned of your having been given away for adoption.

Let me assure you that you were loved and wanted. But circumstances were of such force as to make the adoption necessary. I was shuffled from home to home and probably my childhood was filled with a lot more turmoil than yours as the child of a stable home with loving parents. There were times when I wished someone would love me enough to adopt me. That, however, is water under the bridge. Time and maturity have brought me a depth of understanding which erases any hurt of the past and I hope you will truly realize what a heartbreaking thing it was for Abe and Sarah (I long to call them our parents, but know that you cannot look upon them as your parents just now) to give you up.

I hope too that you will understand how difficult it is to believe that this miracle of finding you has happened. After I read the letter to my dad (he lives with my

22

husband, son and I) I rushed to the phone to call mom. We were both overcome, but mom wants to be sure this wonderful thing is a reality. I hope you will be good enough to answer some questions, so that we can truly rejoice in having found you. I, for one, have been so lonely and longed for my brother.

Can you tell me the address of your home at the time of your adoption? What kind of business was your father in and was he in partnership? You had an aunt who arranged for the adoption. Do you know which one she was, if so please give me her name.

I am overcome with curiosity as to how you learned of your adoption. If this miracle is so, then somehow we must get to see one another. I have so many things to tell you about myself and Abe and Sarah and would want to hear all about you. I understand from a letter my father received from a man in the shop where you went looking for him, that you recently were married. My husband and I have a wonderful son of eleven. It's odd that this should occur, this event of your discovering your adoption. About two years ago my husband and I were in the process of adopting a beautiful little girl. We had her for seven months and then had to give her back to her mother. The circumstances surrounding her having been given up for adoption in the first place were almost parallel to yours, which made it somewhat easier for me to understand the real mother's feelings.

We take hearing from you at this time as an omen of good luck. On Monday my father enters the hospital for surgery. Sarah is remarried now for eight years to a wonderful man. The years have brought peace and understanding to us all. I hope to you too. Please let me hear from you immediately. I am so happy to have found you, dear brother. All my love, Sylvia

23

Sandy was choked up, her eyes moist. When she finished reading, I extended my hand for her to give the letter to me. I read it again, in silence. I got up and went to the kitchen counter and picked up the phone.

"What are you doing?" Sandy asked.

"I'm calling long distance."

"Aren't you going to write?"

"Nope. If I can get the number, I'm going to call." "Operator," the voice said.

"What's the area code for Canoga Park, California?"

"Just a moment...the area code is 213."

"Thank you."

"Long distance, may I help you?" asked another voice.

I gave Sylvia's name and address. "I have no Sylvia, but I have a Max at that address."

"That must be it," I answered.

I dialed...the sound and movement of the rotary dial began. My right index finger continued dialing. Finally, a ring, another ring, another ring. Then a voice from thousands of miles away, and yet so close.

"Hello?"

"Sylvia?"

"Yes."

"This is your brother."

"Oh, my God...you got my letter!"

"Yes."

"How are you?"

"Fine."

There was a short silence. "What do I call you?"

"Sherwin."

"Sherwin...I like that name."

"I don't know, Nathaniel sounds better to me."

24

She laughed. "Tell me all about you. I want to know all about you."

We talked back and forth for a long time. I answered the questions she had asked in her letter: I told her we lived on Wicker Park Avenue, that the aunt who arranged the adoption was probably my mother's sister, and I gave her name. I told her that my father was in partnership with his brothers, in the fruit and vegetable business. Although we didn't run out of things to say, I wanted Sandy to talk to my sister. "Hold the line, I want you to say hello to Sandy."

"Hi, Sylvia, this is Sandy." They talked a long, long time. Sandy was answering questions about me. She made me sound like some movie star. She told Sylvia how tall I was, how handsome I was...I couldn't resist; I took the phone away from her.

"Sylvia," I said, "I'm five-eleven, with shoes on. Everyone's tall next to Sandy; she's only five-one! And if I'm that handsome, how come I didn't make out with all the chicks I dated?" Sylvia laughed. I gave the phone back to Sandy.

While they were talking, my thoughts went over the conversation I had just had with Sylvia. She had told me about trying to find me when she grew older. When I told her I had grown up in Louisville, Kentucky, it made her failure to find me understandable. Sarah was now happily married to a wonderful Irishman, and they lived in Sacramento, California. Sarah had four sisters and four brothers; she was the second child and oldest daughter. Her mother was still alive, and was known as 'The Queen'.

So, I had a grandmother, and I was the oldest grandson. My brother-in-law was an engineer at Lockheed Aircraft. Abe had never remarried, and was retired. I had seventeen first cousins, all living in the Los Angeles area. Many of the aunts and uncles had hit it lucky in business and were living a very comfortable life in the Beverly Hills area. Everyone knew

25

about my letter. I told Sylvia not to tell my name to anyone outside of Abe, Sarah, my brother-in-law and nephew. I explained how I was never told that I was adopted, and that I did not want my parents to know that I knew. We talked about meeting, but put off any exact date. Sandy finally finished talking and gave me back the phone.

"Hi," I said.

"I'll get a letter off with more details," Sylvia promised.

"Good-bye."

"Good-bye, I love you."

"Me, too," I answered softly.

Sandy and I went upstairs to our bedroom. We stayed up late, talking about Sylvia, Sarah, Abe and the rest of the family. We laughed about all the aunts, uncles and cousins in Chicago, and now this gigantic family in California. I wondered what Sarah looked like...I went to sleep with that thought.

One evening the following week, we invited my cousins Deanie, Shirley and their husbands over for refreshments and conversation. I told them that I had found out I was adopted and that I assumed they knew. They did. I told them all the details about finding out, the search and talking to my sister. I told them all I knew, and how I felt about not telling my parents. We talked about Wicker Park. We talked about my sister, Fay, who had died at age seven, how she and Deanie were born days apart, how they had dressed alike and looked like twins, even though my sister had blonde hair and Deanie was a brunette. I had grown up with pictures of Fay and Deanie in the living room and in my parents' bedroom in Chicago and Louisville.

We talked about how, before I was born, when Shirley was not yet two years old, on a winter day when the skies were clear and the sun was bright and the air cool, my aunt had opened a window in the living room. When my mother went

26

into the living room, she yelled back to the kitchen, "Oh, Jennie! Where is Shirley?" No one knew.

My mother became frantic; my aunt became frantic-no Shirley anywhere, and the screenless third-floor window wide open. They ran to the window. Shirley had climbed up on the windowsill and fallen out!

"My God!" they must have screamed. It was just a few years earlier that my sister, Fay, and Shirley and Deanie's sister, Ethel, had died of meningitis within the same week. The speed they must have had running down three flights of stairs, the thoughts and prayers they must have had as they ran out into the front yard! Shirley was crying. She had landed on a large pile of snow that had softened and started to melt from the warm sun...she didn't even have a scratch!

Deanie was beautiful; Shirley was pretty. We were like brother and sisters; we always enjoyed one another's company. Their children were like my nieces and nephews. Nothing had changed...One day I would go to California and meet my sister, Sarah, Abe, my nephew, and all the aunts, uncles and cousins, but I felt no urgency. My family was in Chicago. All of my Wicker Park family, and all of my other aunts, uncles and cousins that I had known all of my life, were in Chicago.

I never called my Aunt Jennie "Aunt Jennie." In the Wicker Park apartment, my mother was always calling to her from one end of the apartment to the other, "Oh, Jennie, Oh, Jennie!" As a kid just learning to speak and distinguish words, I heard it as "Ojeh," and all my life I called her 'Ojeh'. I can remember Ojeh becoming angry with her husband, my Uncle Sam; I can remember her becoming angry with my cousin Shirley; I can remember her becoming angry with her brother, my Uncle Onnie. But with me? Never. Deanie, never. My mother? Never. My father? Never. I can remember my mother becoming angry with my father, my aunt, my two uncles, Shirley and me. But with Deanie? Never.

Our Uncle Onnie was special to Deanie, Shirley and me. He lived with us in Wicker Park, and when I moved to Louisville, he stayed on with the family in Wicker Park. And when they moved to the Northwest Side, on Lyndale Street, Onnie lived there, too. On all the High Holidays, Onnie always sat at the head of the table. At one time, he had studied to be a rabbi, like his father. But he never did become one. Instead, he sold linens at The Boston Store on State Street, in downtown Chicago. A day never went by without his bringing home a toy of some sort for me. "Onnie, Onnie, whatcha got for me, whatcha got?" I'd say. Shirley, I'm sure, got her share of presents, and Deanie did too.

My sister, Fay, had named Onnie. His name was Morris, but Fay couldn't say "uncle," so she would call him "Onnie." The name stuck, and even our friends always called him Onnie.

My life centered around Wicker Park, a four-acre triangular park secluded from the nearby bustle and congestion. We lived directly across from the park, with its benches, bushes and small wading pool, on the quiet street called Wicker Park Avenue.

I can imagine how, perhaps, years ago, small groups of neighboring acquaintances and folks would gather and talk, and then one would say, "Their daughters died last week."

"Whose daughters died last week?"

A bump with the elbow, a nod of the head, a glance, a whisper, "Over there, the Wicker Park family."

I can imagine how, perhaps, years ago, small groups of neighboring acquaintances and folks would gather and talk, and then one would say, "Her sister died."

"Whose sister died?"

A bump with the elbow, a nod of the head, a glance, a whisper, "Over there, the Wicker Park girl."

I can imagine how, perhaps, years ago, small groups of neighboring acquaintances and folks would gather and talk,

28

and then one would say, "She fell out of the third-floor window."

"Who fell out of the third-floor window?"

A bump with the elbow, a nod of the head, a glance, a whisper, "Over there, the Wicker Park child."

I can imagine how, perhaps, years ago, small groups of neighboring acquaintances and folks would gather and talk, and then one would say, "He's adopted."

"Who's adopted?"

The nudge, the nod, the glance, the whisper, "Over there-the Wicker Park Kid!

Chapter 3

The following evening, when Sandy and I returned from the office, we found a letter from Sylvia. It was cold out, so I lit the fireplace. We sat on the couch and opened the letter. A snapshot was enclosed. We studied the picture of Sylvia and my brother-in-law, Max. Sylvia was very attractive. I looked to see if there were any similarities between us. I couldn't find any. I read the letter aloud to Sandy.

November 30, 1961

Dearest Sherwin,

I wonder if you have any idea of how thrilling it was to hear you say "Sylvia, this is your brother." I have been in such a state of excitement since your letter arrived a week ago! Everyone in the family is all steamed up about finding you again and we can hardly wait until you pay us a visit. We have a guest room, ready and waiting for you for as long as you can stay. I am assuming that you've never been to L.A. and plan on showing you all of the sights. We may even take in Las Vegas if there is time. I think that since you are so firm about keeping things from your parents that it is best that I don't come to see you in Chicago, though one of these days I plan on a trip back home to see old friends. We are going to do all that we can to keep things quiet here and except for the immediate family have told no one about you. I'm even keeping your real name a secret from all but Sarah, Abe,

30

my husband Max and my son (who is excellent at keeping a secret).

Barry (your nephew) wants to know if you like sports? He is a baseball fiend and is very proud of the fact that his little league team (with Max as manager) came in second place in Canoga Park area this past summer.

I would like to know as much about you as you care to divulge: were you in the service? Are you a good dancer? What are your favorite foods? What schools did you attend? Do you like to read? Guess I'm very inquisitive, but we have a lot of years to catch up on.

Sarah is so happy, but she isn't quite sure if you care to assume any kind of relationship with her or Abe. Of course she realizes that you can never think of her as more than a stranger, but having read your letter and spoken to you on the phone I have an idea that you are a very compassionate young man and can understand that Sarah does think of you as her son. If you feel that you can, please write to her as a sort of ice breaker. Her address is: Sarah Jamison, 3717 Brownson, Sacramento 21, Calif.

I told you in my last letter that we considered hearing from you as a good luck omen and I was right. It turned out that Abe did not need surgery after all. Sometimes I am so intuitive it scares me because I also had a hunch that you would phone after sending off the letter.

I am going upstairs now and hunt up some snapshots to send to you. Please include some of you and your wife in your reply. To give you an idea of what I look like in person: I'm five foot short, weigh one hundred and five pounds and love to eat! My hair is now a honey blonde and I have hazel green eyes. Barry takes after his father with dark hair and eyes. Hoping to hear from you very soon, I am, Your loving sister, Sylvia

I went back to the part about writing to Sarah. "I couldn't do that," I said.

"What?"

"You know, write to Sarah. I'd feel like I was cheating on my mother." Sandy agreed, and went upstairs.

I sat on the bear rug in front of the fireplace. It felt good. My thoughts were on Sarah. I wondered, again, what she looked like now. I tried to visualize what she had looked like when I was born. I didn't think about Abe; I thought about Sylvia, but mostly about Sarah. I just wasn't ready to make a trip out to California now. I had just gotten married, my business was young, and I couldn't afford to take time off work.

It was getting colder. The coach house was almost impossible to heat, with its high ceiling and all that marble and tile. I figured Sandy must be under the covers wearing a sweater. I turned out the lights and went upstairs.

"It's c-c-cold," Sandy quivered. I hurriedly got undressed and put on a sweater and got under the covers with Sandy.

I chattered, "You're r-r-right, it's cold!" We snuggled, warming our bodies. "This is ridiculous," we agreed. The owner of the building had already sent someone over, twice, about the heat. The furnace was just too small for the coach house. We wondered what things would be like when January and February came around.

I was just starting to get warmed up under the covers, when the phone rang. I reached over to the nightstand and picked up the receiver. "Hello?"

"Sherwin, Edward," the voice said.

"Ed, how are you? Are you and Vicki back in Chicago?"

"No, we'll be back in a few days, and we were wondering if we could stay with you and Sandy until my interview at Bell & Howell on Monday."

"Sure, no problem." I turned to Sandy and repeated the conversation.

"Great," Sandy agreed.

"So, you're not going to take that job in New York?" I asked him.

"I don't know yet. I want to see what Bell & Howell has to offer."

"Here, I'll let you talk to Sandy and she wants to talk to Vicki...Take care, I'll see you soon." I handed the phone to Sandy.

Ed and Vicki were close friends. We had met them at a party shortly after Sandy and I had started dating. Ed was a physicist. He was hooked on an injectable prescription medication. His wife was taking the drug, too, but not to the degree Ed was. They had offered it to us, and at first, we were both hesitant because of the needle. But we tried it and found it very enjoyable. The four of us had stayed up all night, talking. Despite having had no sleep I remember doing a full day's work, selling, the next day. I'd had a good day. In fact, it was a great sales day. I thought, "Gee, I hope Ed brings some of that stuff with him."

That weekend, Vicki and Ed arrived. They had never been to the coach house before, but had been looking forward to it, especially after Sandy's description of its uniqueness. We hugged and kissed and showed them around and up to their bedroom. I had the fireplace going, and we returned downstairs and sat in front of the fire and talked.

Ed and Vicki did not drink alcohol, so I offered them a soft drink or coffee. Ed followed me to the kitchen, and watched as I started to make martinis for Sandy and me. "Sherwin, Vicki and I are going to have some Meth, and if you and Sandy want some, don't drink."

"Sandy, I'm going to have some Meth with Vicki and Ed. You want to join us?"

"Sure."

"Then do you want coffee or Coke? Because we can't have alcohol."

"I'll take coffee," Sandy replied. I poured the drinks and carried them to the fireplace. I threw another log on the fire.

Ed went upstairs to retrieve the Methedrine and his little black toiletry bag that held his paraphernalia. He returned, and the three of us watched as he went through the same ritual Sandy and I had witnessed for the first time five months ago. He opened the box of vials manufactured by the drug company, Burroughs Wellcome. The name of the drug was methamphetamine hydrochloride, sold under the brand name Methedrine. It was packaged a hundred vials to a box, and this box was half empty.

Ed spread the alcohol, cotton, syringe and needles on top of a black cloth napkin. "Ed, let me read that poop sheet in the box," I asked. He handed it to me, and I started skimming it and reading some of it aloud to Sandy. "Sandy, you read it; I can't even pronounce some of these words," I laughed. Sandy always amazed me with how she could pronounce all the words in the Merck Medical Manual we had in our bookcase. She impressed me with her vast knowledge of the English language. I always tried to trip her up with the definition of words in the dictionary; I never could. She always beat me and our friends at Scrabble. She was an avid reader of novels.

I handed Sandy the small, folded white information sheet marked "For the Profession Only," and listened attentively as she read aloud:

"Methedrine brand Methamphetamine Hydrochloride. Injection. 20 mg in 1 cc."

There must have been more than a thousand words describing its various medical uses, ranging from the drug's use in operative procedures for the purpose of maintaining blood pressure or restoring it to normal, to its value as an analeptic in the treatment of coma resulting from alcoholism or an overdose of sedatives or hypnotics, as in barbiturate poisoning. Sandy also read the precautions for patients with irregularities in cardiac rhythm or severe hypertension.

But the part I found most interesting was the description of the drug's action as a cortical stimulant, producing euphoria and increased mental clarity and a change in behavior "consisting of restlessness and over talkativeness" accompanied by a "profound" recall and production of a "free flow of emotionally charged material" lasting up to several hours. "Most patients," it went on to say, "experience a dramatic relief from tension and a feeling of relaxation."

"Ed, how did you get a prescription for this?" I asked.

"The psychiatrist I was seeing a few years ago used it to help me to verbalize and get my feelings out, and I started using it on my own to be able to stay alert during hours of research. He gives me a prescription whenever I want."

Watching Ed, I was curious. "Why are there two different-size needles?"

"The short one is for the arm, the long one is for the ass," he answered. "Do you want to try the long one?"

I hesitated. I remembered that the first time Sandy and I had tried the drug, he'd had only the short needles. "Yeah," I bravely responded. Ed asked Sandy which she preferred, and she chose the short needle; so did Vicki.

I asked Ed about sterilizing everything, and, because he really liked to explain thoroughly, he smiled and launched into teaching me all about it.

"Well, these are all new needles, never been used, so I'll sterilize them with this little bottle of rubbing alcohol. Later, I'll boil them in water. When they become dull, I'll buy new ones. The syringe I flush with water, then alcohol."

We all watched as he snapped the head off the long-necked vial with his thumb. He drew the fluid through the sterilized needle into the syringe. Holding the syringe upright, he meticulously checked for air bubbles, as a few drops of Meth squirted out of the needle. Satisfied, he rubbed Vicki's upper arm with a small piece of cotton, wet with alcohol, and injected the Methedrine intramuscularly. He repeated the procedure for Sandy.

"Did it hurt?" I asked.

Sandy smiled. "No, and it didn't hurt the last time, either."

Then Ed turned to me and requested that I lie down on my stomach and pull my pants and shorts down. I obeyed, and he rubbed the wet cotton on a spot he chose on my rear end. He injected the drug through the long needle.

"There, did that hurt?" he asked.

"No...just a little." I pulled up my pants and sat up to watch Ed. He pulled down his pants and shorts, twisted sideways and injected himself. Sandy and I found that to be interesting.

We talked and waited for the drug to take effect, less than twenty minutes. Ed explained that a psychiatrist would give Meth intravenously to his patients. The drug would work within five minutes, that way. Ed and Vicki never took it intravenously.

"How much do you guys take a day?"

"I take about five cc's a day," Ed answered.

"What's a 'cc'?" I asked.

"One vial," Vicki answered.

"How much do you take?" I asked Vicki.

"About three vials a day,"

"How do you guys ever sleep?" I asked.

"Well, we don't take it every day," Vicki said.

"But how do you ever sleep when you do take it?"

"If we want to sleep, we'll take Placidyl," Vicki explained.

"What's Placidyl?" I asked.

"It's a drug for insomnia," Sandy answered.

"Do you inject that?" I asked.

"No," Vicki laughed. "It's a capsule."

"Oh," I said.

The drug was starting to work. I felt good. I looked at Sandy, and I could tell she was feeling good, too. The feeling was one of euphoria-of well-being. I got up and put three more logs on the fire.

"What are you doing?" Sandy asked.

"I'm building a fire," I said. They all laughed.

I sat behind Sandy, on the floor in front of the fireplace, and rolled up the sleeves of her sweater and gently rubbed her arms. I was in a loving mood.

I told Vicki and Ed about my adoption. They were fascinated with the story. We talked for about four hours.

"Do you want another shot?" Ed asked us.

"Sure," I said.

"Sure," Sandy said.

"Sure," Vicki said.

Ed repeated his ritual as we waited our turns for the injection. It was after midnight, and we talked for a while longer.

I kissed Sandy on the cheek. "Let's go upstairs," I whispered in her ear.

"Okay," she said.

I picked her up. Her long black hair fell over my arms. She had a tiny waist, beautiful breasts. I was through talking.

"We'll see you guys tomorrow," I said. Ed and Vicki smiled.

I carried my 103-pound package up the winding marble staircase.

Sex was incredible that night. We didn't get to sleep until almost four hours later. Sandy and I woke up about noon. We felt fine. Ed and Vicki were still sleeping.

We left them a note on the staircase and we went to see my folks.

That evening, the four of us ate take-out Chinese food. We sat around the fireplace and ate and talked. We didn't do Meth. The following morning, Sandy went to the office, Ed and Vicki left, and I went out selling.

Several months had passed. Besides the rent for the coach house being high, the heating bills were absurd. We decided we weren't going to be working to support the coach house. We broke the lease and rented a two-bedroom apartment in a six-flat on Montrose Avenue, near Lake Michigan. There were two apartments to a floor, and we had interesting neighbors.

We lived on the first floor. Our next-door neighbor was a widow who lived alone. Her apartment was from out of the past; all the furniture was from the 1920s. She made costumes for a belly dancer who called herself Sheba. I saw them both a few times.

Above us were a mother, her daughter, and her sister. The daughter, Bobbie, was in her early twenties. She was always visiting us. She was a go-go dancer, and fun to be with. Next door to the three women was a newly married couple from France. Talking with them gave me a chance to brush up on my French. It was totally different from our coach house on Burton Place. There, we hadn't known our neighbors. Sandy and I had now settled into a conventional Chicago lifestyle.

We saw my folks every weekend, and the rest of my Wicker Park family every other weekend. We occasionally saw the other aunts, uncles and cousins. We kept in touch with my sister Sylvia.

In bits and pieces, I learned more about the family in California, about Sarah, about Abe. About why and how I was given up for adoption. Between my sister in California and my cousins in Chicago, the story unfolded.

The year was 1928. My sister Fay was seven when she died in the hospital of meningitis. Doctors were like gods, and my parents had the best, but medicines that cured were unknown

38

then. It was a dreaded disease. Prayer didn't help. Their beautiful and only child was gone; only memories were left. It wasn't fair, it wasn't right. Fay was their whole life.

Five days earlier, my mother's sister's youngest daughter, Ethel, had died. She was three years old. The same hospital, the same doctors, the same disease. The wailing at the cemetery, the wailing at home, must have touched the souls of all who were there.

Poor Deanie, she was only seven. She and Fay had been inseparable. Now, within the same week, she had lost her baby sister, too. How could these indelible impressions ever go away? I don't know; I never asked Deanie.

Months later, my cousin Shirley was born. My parents were like parents to Deanie and Shirley. Both families still lived together in the same apartment in Wicker Park.

My mother tried to get pregnant; she couldn't. The doctor told her she couldn't have any more children. My aunt probably felt guilty. She had two children; my parents had none. Sure, Deanie and Shirley were like theirs, but it wasn't the same. They wanted Fay, but that couldn't be. They wanted their own child. They wanted their own to love.

Three years later and miles away, in another section of Chicago, Abe and Sarah had separated. They had a four-year-old daughter, Sylvia. Sarah had an older brother, three younger brothers, and four younger sisters. Some of the brothers and sisters were married; others lived at home with Sarah's widowed mother. Life was a struggle for Abe...times were not good. Making a living was difficult. Sarah was free-spirited. She loved to act, sing and dance, all of which she did on the stage of Chicago's Yiddish Theatre. Abe disapproved. They had a child; Sarah's place was at home. Acting, singing, and dancing were not proper. Sarah's sisters, brothers and mother sided with Abe.

Sarah wanted to do what she wanted to do: life was to enjoy. No one could change her mind. The Yiddish Theatre was where her friends were- that was where she belonged, that was what was the most important. She wanted it all-her friends, the theater, Sylvia and Abe. She could share; it was Abe who could not. One day, while they were separated, she stopped by Abe's apartment. In the heat of passion, they had sex, and I was conceived.

As the months went by, Abe avoided his family responsibilities. He was unemployed. Sylvia had been sent to live with an aunt, one of Sarah's sisters. No one had any money; another mouth to feed was impossible. Sarah, with the help of a friend, rented a small room in an apartment building and kept me in a dresser drawer. She didn't have any way to heat a bottle for me; she had no money and very little time to tend to me, so she put me in a Catholic boarding home. When she wasn't able to pay for my care, she was threatened with being turned over to the authorities and my becoming a ward of the State.

Sarah's older brother had always given her moral support. He ran an inexpensive classified ad in The Jewish Daily Forward, a Yiddish newspaper. The year was 1932. My aunt saw the ad for a wealthy family to adopt, provide for and love a six-week-old baby boy. She made arrangements to meet Sarah's brother. Together, they went to the Catholic home to see me. Years ago, my aunt had told Deanie about how sickly and skinny I looked, about the rashes and sores on my body. My aunt told my parents-to-be how I looked, that all I would need would be good care and I would be fine. She told them that the man who had placed the ad was tall, handsome and healthy, and that the man had said his sister was beautiful. He said they did not want any money for the baby, just the sixty dollars that was owed to the Catholic home. They just wanted to be sure that I would be given to a loving family who could provide.

There was no hesitation by the Wicker Park family. Sarah's brother was given the sixty dollars, and he and my aunt brought me back to Wicker Park. He assured everyone that his sister would never come to take me away. The Wicker Park family retained an attorney. I was named after my new mother's father, the rabbi. I was officially adopted at three months of age.

I can imagine how my Wicker Park family must have spoken, in Yiddish, to He On High, during the grieving years: "Oh God, oh God, why me? Why us? We always lived the laws of the Torah, we always listened to you. Oh, God, why, why, why? We kept a kosher home. We always went to the synagogue. We always obeyed your commandments. Oh, God, oh, God. Why, why, why, why? My child, my child, my Fay, my Fay. Please, oh God, give me back my child, give me back my child." My mother and father must have wept those words hundreds of times. My uncles, my aunt and Deanie...oh, how they all must have wept for the two little girls.

And now, in a mysterious way, God had answered the prayers of my Wicker Park family. Perhaps, too, God had answered the prayers of Sarah.

Chapter 4

I pushed the thought of meeting my California family out of my mind. I was totally involved with growing my business, and I was putting in long hours every day. Several months later, I received a letter from Sylvia.

Feb. 14, 1962

Dear Sherwin,

I've debated writing this letter to you for weeks, but with both our birthdays approaching I kind of got sentimental and decided that I had to find out why you haven't written. It's very disconcerting to have found my brother and then to have him leave me again. I don't know what your reasons are, but believe me if you really feel that you would prefer to forget that you ever found me I will respect your wishes. Only won't you be kind enough to write and tell me so.

I hope that you and your loved ones have been well. We have had two losses recently, my grandfather and a very dear aunt. Everyone (family only) has asked me repeatedly what news I have from you and I have had to say "nothing at all." Please write soon and take care of yourself.

Your sister, Sylvia

P.S. I want you to know that your visit to my father's shop in Chicago led to talk and if your parents found out that you are aware of having been adopted it did not come from here. It isn't easy to keep those things a secret.

I waited the few days and called her on our birthday, the twenty-second of February. She was relieved and happy to hear from me. I told her that I just wasn't able to make the trip yet, and we let it go at that.

Spring had arrived in Chicago. The snow had all melted. April has always been like the start of the new year for me; it's my favorite month, even with its showers.

Occasionally, you would get snow in April. But April was special; you could usually put away your rubber boots, your heavy coats. The temperature, no longer freezing, was usually in the low fifties and you knew the next month would bring warm breezes from Lake Michigan that would make spring more sudden than April in Paris.

In the spring, old friends would come out of the woodwork. One day I got a call from my friend Don. Don was a single, tall, handsome, blonde Swede. He was always with a different girl. Don would take a pill to get up in the morning, another pill midday, another pill before hitting the bar scene, and a final pill before going to bed. Don and I had a thing going with a twenty-dollar bill. He would borrow twenty dollars from me, and a week or so later, he would repay the debt. A few weeks later, he would borrow twenty dollars from me again. This time, he was six months late.

"Sherwin!"

"Don," I answered.

I told him that Sandy and I were married. He was happy for us. Don was always happy. He got my address and came over to repay the twenty dollars.

Sandy, Don and I sat around talking. I told him about this great injectable drug, Methedrine. "A friend of ours takes it all the time, but he took a job out of state, and I never see him anymore."

Don was interested. Several months ago, he had met this gal in a bar. They became good friends. She was a lesbian. She took Methedrine injectably. Don would never try it that way; he was afraid of needles, but he had taken it in pill form. Don told Sandy and me that we would have to meet this gal. Her name was Geri, she was from New York, she was Jewish. "She's really funny," he laughed.

A few nights later, Don brought Geri over to our apartment. Geri, who was in her mid-twenties, did not look like a butch, nor was she a "femme fatale." She looked like a tomboy. We sat around, we talked, we joked. It was a fun evening. Don, I'm sure, was high on pills. Geri, I'm sure, had had her Meth; she was really witty.

Geri lived in a one-room apartment with her girlfriend, Boots, a stripper, who was on the road most of the time. They had a cat. Geri had invented a decorative three-panel screen to be placed in front of the cat's litter box to hide it. She wanted to manufacture the screen and was looking for an investor. I told her I might be interested.

The next day, I went over to Geri's small studio apartment on the Near North Side.

She showed me the screen and gave me drawings to take back for Sandy to see. She offered me Meth. I accepted.

She gave me a pop in the arm. We sat around on the floor and talked. She told me how she had met Don. She and Boots were sitting on stools in a local bar. Don walked in; she heard his pills rattle in his pocket. "You're rattling," Geri said to him. Don laughed, and the three of them ordered Cokes and became friends.

44

Geri was a prostitute, a call girl. She had just a few select clients, mostly married couples from out of town. Occasionally, she had Don go with her on special requests. Geri worked maybe two or three times a month. I tried to imagine her dressed up in a dress; I couldn't! Years ago, Geri had been on hard drugs in New York before quitting cold turkey. She would never go back to that; Meth was just fine, she told me.

I went back home, showed Sandy the drawings, and told her about Geri. I told her I had had a shot. We decided that we would invest up to eight hundred dollars in the screen project for twenty per cent of the profits. The first eight hundred dollars to come in would repay our investment. We were too busy with the insurance business to become more involved beyond that. We called Geri, and we all agreed on the arrangement. Geri was all hung up on her cat screens; they were her gift to mankind.

One day Sandy and I stopped by Geri's apartment. Boots was there; she was in town for a week. We each had a pop in the arm. Geri had a prescription for Methedrine, and a drugstore a few blocks away would deliver. It was forty dollars for a box of one hundred vials. Boots never took the drug when she was out of town. Geri took it all the time.

Sandy wasn't concerned about becoming hooked; she always disliked the feeling the next day after the drug wore off and she had had little or no sleep. She couldn't understand how our friends Ed, Vicki and, now, Geri, could take as much as they did.

One day soon after that I called Geri and asked if she could "get some of that stuff for me and all the things that go with it."

"Sure," she said.

I went over to the apartment; Boots was out of town. We sat on the floor and had a pop. She ordered a box, needles, syringe, cotton and alcohol for me. In an hour, the doorbell rang; it was our order. I paid the delivery boy. I had Geri go over the whole procedure, step by step, with me. She taught me how to clear the syringe for air bubbles. She was fast, not like Ed and his slow ritual.

I left carrying my purchases in a shopping bag. I was a little paranoid, walking to my car. I didn't have a prescription.

I went back to our apartment and showed Sandy the goodies. She was apprehensive. "Don't worry," I said, "I'm not going to get hooked on it."

I laid everything out on top of the bedroom dresser. I went through the slow ritual, the same as Ed had. I rubbed Sandy's arm with the alcohol-soaked cotton and gave her a shot. I taught her how to do it, and Sandy gave me a shot in the arm. We got undressed and lay in bed, talking.

We talked about Sandy's life, her loves; we talked about my life, my loves. Our talk and feelings were deeper than we had ever expressed. We talked about my adoption. Hours later, we made love.

I was stopping by Geri's apartment two or three times a week. I always had a shot of Methedrine there; then I would come home and give myself a shot. I was doing Meth about three times a week, about nine cc's a week. Sandy and I would do it together about once every two weeks. A lot of repressed feelings started to emerge. I started to analyze my life. I recalled instances with my parents where I had, or hadn't, done certain things. I experienced guilt. I analyzed Sarah and Abe. I couldn't understand why they had given me away. I cried a lot, falling asleep in Sandy's arms.

After a while, I was up to six cc's a day, every day. I slept little. I got Placidyls from Geri to counteract the Meth so I could sleep. Sandy didn't know I was doing six vials a day.

Repressed feelings always emerged. I was going through a self-analytical process. Buried memories came forth, buried guilt came forth. Analytical insight about people and situations came easily. An outflow of tears and emotions became a daily occurrence. Many a night I would cry myself to sleep in Sandy's arms. "How could she have given me away, how could she have given me away?" I asked and wept. I hated her, I wanted her...I was all fucked up!

One day, Sandy returned from the office to find me lying on my back on the living room couch. I was having trouble breathing; I was having trouble catching my breath.

The feeling of euphoria was gone. There was a feeling of toxicity throughout my head.

The shortness of breath was a horrible feeling. I swore that if this feeling of horror left, I would never, ever take Meth again.

"Sherwin, what's wrong?"

"I took too much Meth."

"Should I call a doctor?"

"No! I'll be alright; just let me rest." I had my arm flung over my forehead. Sandy looked at me and left the room. She trusted my judgment.

Later that evening, I regained my ability to take deep breaths, and my breathing was normal again. I got up from the couch. Sandy was reading in bed. I retrieved the box of Methedrine, the syringe and needles from a comer of my dresser drawer. I left the door open from our bedroom to the bathroom. Sandy watched as I snapped the heads off the Methedrine vials and threw them, one by one, into the toilet. Three flushes, and the box was empty. I cracked the syringe, broke the needles and threw them into the bathroom wastebasket. I stood in the doorway and looked at Sandy. "Never again," I vowed. "That stuff sucks!"

Months went by. It was now fall. Directly across the street from our apartment were Quonset huts that were being used as classrooms for the overflow from the public school. To the right was a small open, grassy area with trees around it. The leaves had started to change colors, and soon they would drop.

I had seen Geri several times but had totally given up on Meth. I advanced her the money I promised for the cat screens, and she did her thing.

Sandy and I had never discussed her getting pregnant. We had always been careful. Once we were careless. It took just once. The day she came home from the doctor, she glowed.

"I'm pregnant," she announced.

"Are you sure?"

"The doctor said yes."

I smiled. I was happy. But there was a feeling of Permanence. Adulthood. Responsibility. I had never had to face those things before. I pushed the thought of Sandy's pregnancy out of my mind as often as I could.

As the weeks passed, I became more conscious of her pregnancy. I counted all the aunts, uncles and cousins in Chicago. I counted all the aunts, uncles and cousins in California. I thought about my mother and father. I thought about Sarah, Abe and Sylvia. Now Sandy was pregnant, and a whole new lineage was about to start. I didn't know where I fit in this whole scheme of things. I didn't know me.

Sandy wasn't home yet. I picked up the phone and dialed. "Hello," the groggy voice answered.

"Geri," I said

"Sherwin." Her voice became cheerful.

"You going to be home? I want to come over."

"Sure," she said.

My usual two soft knocks on her door; I was in. We sat on the floor. When I had gotten off Meth before, Geri had never asked why, and she had never offered it again.

"Can I have some Meth?" I asked.

"Sure," she replied.

"Geri, you got any of those long needles?"

"Yeah, do you know how to use them?"

"Yes."

48

Geri gave herself a pop in the arm. She handed me the syringe and a long needle. I snapped the head off the vial with my thumb. I fed the Meth through the needle, up into the syringe. I heard the *swoosh* of the last drop as it was sucked up. I held the syringe upright and pushed the plunger in, until a few drops squirted out, and the marking on the syringe showed the fluid level at one cc. I checked for air bubbles. I excused myself and went into the bathroom. I pulled down my pants and shorts, rubbed the alcohol-wet cotton on an upper spot of my ass and gave myself a shot. I felt the twinge and depth of the needle. It didn't hurt. It felt good. My thumb pressed down on the top of the syringe and I slowly let the Meth slip into my body.

I sat back down on the floor. We talked. After a while, all tension was gone. I was relaxed. I felt real good.

"Geri, how do I get my own prescription?"

She wouldn't give me the name of her doctor, but she gave me the name and address of a doctor whose office wasn't too far from my apartment.

"I understand you can get just about anything from him," she told me.

I returned to my apartment. I didn't tell Sandy anything about the Meth, or about my visit to Geri's apartment. I made it a point not to be too talkative. Sandy did not suspect.

The next day, I went to the doctor's office. It was a small, dingy office. There were two male patients ahead of me. The receptionist gave me a form to fill out. I gave it back to her, only partially filled out.

"Why do you want to see the doctor?" she asked.

"It's personal," I answered.

I went into the doctor's office. I introduced myself and explained that I wanted a prescription for injectable Methedrine.

49

"Methedrine, Methedrine...I never heard of that one," he said. He got up from his chair and returned to his desk with a large book.

"Let's see, Methedrine. Oh, here it is," he murmured. He skimmed the information in the medical book. "Why do you want this?"

"I've taken it before, and it relieves me of tension."

He called for his assistant to take me into the examining room and take my blood pressure. He came in and listened to my heartbeat with his stethoscope and he took my pulse. We returned to his office. He wrote me out a prescription.

"I'll need some syringes and needles, too...long and short," I added.

"Okay," he said. "Pay my assistant on the way out."

I paid my twenty dollars. I now had my own prescription. No paranoia, it was all legal. I went to the drugstore near my apartment. The pharmacist recognized me from previous shopping. I handed him the prescription.

"Methedrine, Methedrine ...someone asked about that a month ago. I don't carry it. If you come back in a couple of hours, I'll have it. I have to get it from another store."

"Sure," I said.

I returned later, and my prescription, plus syringes and needles, was ready. I bought rubbing alcohol and cotton.

"What do they use that drug for?" the pharmacist asked.

"Tension...tension," I answered.

Sunday, we went to my folks' apartment. All the Wicker Park family was there, except for Deanie and Shirley. They were all delighted by Sandy's pregnancy.

My mother brought out two shoe boxes of pictures to show Sandy. There were pictures of my sister Fay; pictures of my cousin Ethel; pictures of Deanie, Shirley, my Uncle Sam, Onnie, Ojeh. Pictures of my parents, and naturally, lots and lots of pictures of me.

I studied my mother, father, aunt and uncles. It was difficult to comprehend that my mother had not given birth to me. But I really didn't look like anyone else in the family. I was remembering how, as a kid, I would kiss Ojeh, I would kiss Onnie, I would kiss my father. I would kiss my Uncle Sam whenever I returned to Chicago or left to go back to Louisville. Then I realized that as a kid, I had never kissed my mother; she had always kissed me -except for that one time in Louisville, when I was not yet seven. It was a Saturday afternoon at the Rex Theater on Fourth Street. I had done something bad, and my mother was very upset with me. I felt awful. I had just realized today, twenty-four years later, that at the time, I must have felt I was being rejected. We made up in the theater, and I kissed my mother.

Driving home, Sandy remarked how, in all the pictures of me next to my mother, I was always pulling away. We laughed.

That evening I gave myself a shot in the arm, in the bathroom, in secrecy. I was doing two shots a day, alternating between the arm and the ass, about three times a week. I felt good, and my work performance was excellent. My insight and perception were clear and constant. I was in control.

As the months passed, and Sandy's pregnancy showed, I began to increase my dosage. The outpouring of emotions increased during the late evenings. We stayed up every night and talked a lot. I had always answered Sylvia's letters with a phone call. I quit calling. I was stopping by Geri's apartment frequently. I rarely ate. I rarely slept.

I would stop taking Methedrine for several weeks, and then I would start up again.

We skipped going to my folks' house every Sunday. I would sleep through the day.

One night, Sandy found an empty vial that hadn't gone down the toilet. She confronted me. We fought, we argued. She cried.

"You bastard!" she screamed.

51

I paused, I smiled. "You know, maybe you've got something there."

Sandy made me promise to go with her to see her obstetrician, Dr. Benensohn, with whom she had a close relationship. He made her feel that she was his favorite patient.

She had told him about my adoption. I had met him one time, when I had gone with Sandy to his office. He seemed quite nice.

"All right, call him up. I'll go with you," I snapped.

Dr. Benensohn's reception room was busy. Sandy told me his office was always like that. We went into his private office. His ashtray was full and he held a lit cigarette; he was a chain-smoker.

We talked about Sandy, about her pregnancy, about the baby. Everything was fine; her due date was in late May. Dr. Benensohn talked about the pressure of his practice and his addiction to four packs of cigarettes a day, plus endless cups of coffee. We talked about Methedrine and its effects. He told me that I was apparently addicted to it and that I should stop. We spent twenty minutes talking. We all stood up. Dr. Benensohn put his arms around Sandy and assured her everything would turn out all right.

"Don't worry, Sherwin will stop taking the drug. I have confidence in him," he said.

He shook my hand and walked us to the reception area.

"Thanks very much for your time. I appreciate it, Dr. Benensohn," I said.

Sandy and I stopped in a restaurant and ordered coffee. She was somber, but reassured by our conversation with Dr. Benensohn.

I told her I had a prescription for Methedrine. I explained that I hadn't told her because I knew she wouldn't approve, and I didn't want to hurt her.

"How much are you taking?" she asked.

"Two a day," I lied.

"Every day?"

"No-o-o...not every day." I grinned.

I told her how I had gotten the prescription and that all my vital signs checked out fine.

"You know, I'm not ready to give it up just now, and I don't want to have to sneak," I said.

Sandy hesitated, thinking. "You know, I'm not going to take any while I'm pregnant," she said.

"I know that," I responded.

"Even after the baby, I don't think I want that stuff again," she added. I agreed. I dropped her off at the apartment, and I went out selling.

Later that evening, I prepared a shot in front of Sandy. I used the long needle. She shook her head. "I can't believe you're doing that."

"I'm pretty good," I answered. She went to bed and read.

I pulled the cardboard backing out of some shirts that had come back from the laundry. I wrote and I wrote and I wrote.

"What are you doing?" Sandy asked me.

"I'm writing."

"I can see that. What are you writing?"

"My feelings."

"Your what?"

"My feelings...you know, my emotions. You don't want to talk. I just took Meth; I feel like talking. I can't, so I'm writing."

Sandy cracked up. We hugged. Everything was OK.

I got up the next morning, feeling good. I had gotten about four hours sleep. I dropped Sandy off at the office and went out selling. I felt good that the ice was broken and I didn't have to sneak. I had done a lot of thinking the previous night, while Sandy slept. It was very obvious to me that discovering I was adopted and now Sandy's being pregnant was just a lot of heavy stuff happening at once. I had thought about Sarah's being pregnant with me, about how she and Abe were separated, about nobody wanting me. Was I reliving my own embryonic feelings of rejection while encased in Sarah's womb? It was an interesting observation, I thought. I thought about Sandy and me. If we were separated, and in the process of getting a divorce. If she got pregnant, if we had no money? I couldn't have done that, no, I couldn't have done that. Unless, unless, I thought, I felt I wasn't the father. I had a burning desire to know as much about Sarah as possible.

Later, alone at the apartment, I started to think of Sarah. From Sylvia's letters and our conversations, I knew quite a bit about Sarah. She was twenty-four when I was born. She was separated from Abe. She was beautiful, and she loved to dance and sing. She used to sing "Yiddishe Momme" on the Jewish Hour radio program in Chicago. She acted and danced in the Yiddish Theatre in Chicago. I remember going there on Sundays, when we lived in Wicker Park. The theater was on Chicago's West Side, on Roosevelt Road. I remember everyone sitting on the hard wooden folding chairs. I remember being frustrated because I didn't understand the words. I remember the lively music, dancing and costumes. I used to wish I understood; I wanted them to speak English. I remember the acting with all the facial expressions and body language. I could understand bits and pieces, just by the actors' inflections and expressions. God, it was frustrating not to understand those guttural sounds. I liked the rhythm of the language. I remembered the beautiful feminine voice singing "Yiddishe Momme" on the Jewish Hour. I remember the entire Wicker Park family sitting in silence in the dining room, listening to the radio, listening to the song. Everyone loved that song. My parents, aunt, and uncles must have always thought of their mothers when that song was sung. I remember that they would just sit and stare off into the distance. Tears would roll down the women's cheeks; the men's eyes would get watery. "My God!" I thought, "I bet that was Sarah!"

I walked into the bathroom. I braced myself against the sink. I looked in the mirror. My eyes were red, my eyes were tearing. My cheeks were puffed, my throat was choked. I looked in the mirror, and I bawled.

After a while, I wiped away my tears. I bent over the sink and filled my palms with the cold running water. I wet my face from my forehead down to my neck. I grabbed a towel and wiped my face. I went into the other room, got my Meth and popped my arm.

When Sandy came home, I told her what had happened. She held back tears. I kissed her on the lips, and we went out to talk and eat.

We went to Sandy's favorite Chinese restaurant near the apartment. Since being pregnant, she'd had a craving for wonton soup. Two bowls for her was the usual. We returned to the apartment and Sandy brought in the mail. There was a letter from Sylvia.

February 24, 1963

Dear Sherwin,

I was very surprised and very happy to receive your note. To be perfectly honest I had the feeling that you would rather leave things as they are, with the knowledge that we are brother and sister, but not pursuing it any further. Needless to say I want very much to see you.

Which brings me to the reason for this letter, aside from thanking you. On June 29th our son is being bar-mitzvahed and nothing would please all of us more than to have you and Sandy be here with us on this very important occasion. If there is any possibility and if you feel that it won't be too awkward for you, please make

*some arrangements to come out here. Will be waiting to
hear from you either way.*

Love, Sylvia

"I should call her," I said.

"Yes," Sandy agreed.

I called Sylvia. It felt good saying hello and hearing her
voice. She was happy that I had not deserted her. I reassured
her that everything was fine. I explained that Sandy was
pregnant and that I was preoccupied now, but looked forward
to meeting her sometime after the baby was born. I explained
that we wouldn't come to her son's Bar Mitzvah, because I
would probably end up being the center of attention. It wasn't
right, I thought; that was my nephew's day. I couldn't do that.
Besides, except for a few close friends, I had always been the
quiet type. I jokingly said that Sandy's being pregnant was
having a big effect on me. I got her to laugh. I gave the phone
to Sandy, and they talked a long time.

The weeks and months passed. In May, I received another
letter from Sylvia. Many of the things she said about Sarah I
already knew from previous phone conversations.

May 24, 1963

Dearest Sherwin,

*It was really wonderful talking to you. From what I
can tell in just our conversation, you are very definitely
my brother ..... that is, we are alike in many ways. My
friends lovingly (?) refer to me as a NUT. That is to say
that I am as nonconforming as possible without being
considered an offbeat character. I'm no bohemian, far
from it. But I am not one to go along with the crowd just*

56

for the sake of being accepted. You sound as though you too have a mind of your own, the only kind to have.

As to my writing, procrastination is the main reason I haven't finished a novel I started years ago (one of which I can be proud, that is). The two paperbacks that were published were a very commercial venture and I am reluctant to even discuss them.

After all, how does a mother of a nearly thirteen year old boy excuse the writing of erotic romance novels, even if she is a nonconformist.

Like my mother I also have a flair for dramatics. I've studied little theatre at the nearby junior college and at one time acting was my primary goal in life. Sarah was on the Jewish Hour for a long time, singing under the name of Sonia Gable and she also appeared on the Jewish theatre circuit. She had a lovely voice and a lot of talent, but at the time with their narrow minded prejudice their aunts and uncles pointed a finger of shame at her and she was forced to give it up.

Of course my father, Abe, felt the same way and I believe this was the biggest cause of trouble. At least it led to the breakup, his lack of insight to her needs. Mother was a very outgoing, bubbly type of person. She loved to sing and dance. She was a wonderful cook, still is but she wanted more out of life than what women of that age felt was a woman's lot. My father had very little understanding then.

He's come a long way since and it's amazing to see how he now enjoys playing cards where once he thought my mother scandalous for an occasional game of poker. Oh well, that is water under the bridge I suppose. It made for a very mixed up childhood though and as a result I have been trying to find myself for years. I am finally making headway.

After your call last week I discussed you with my therapist and began to realize how much losing my brother had a bearing on the shaping of my personality. I am looking forward to meeting you, to getting acquainted with you and I know that I will love you because you are my brother.

My book will be in the mail to you soon, but remember this is not representative of my ability as a writer nor of me as a person. Hope that Sandy is well and that all goes right for her when the baby arrives. I told Barry that you feel it wouldn't be right to take away from him on what you termed "his day", but he said that he wouldn't care, that he would like you to be here for the Bar Mitzvah. He has written to you about it. Sarah said that should you decide to come in, you could arrange to see each other ahead of time so she can be all cried out by the time the big day arrives. She realizes that you have very little feelings for her, but as a mother herself I can understand how she longs to see you ....even if you are strangers. However, the decision is yours.

If you don't come here and still want me to visit you then we will plan on that. I would rather wait until the weather is cool though and Barry is back in school. About the middle of September or thereabouts would be best, probably after the High Holidays.

Stay well dear and as to this baby bit, believe me, after a while you will really dig it!

Love, Sylvia

Sandy had stopped working at the office. Her mother came from Denver to stay with us just prior to Sandy's due date. I always enjoyed my mother-in-law's company. She knew of my adoption, and she never talked about it, unless I brought it up.

She never offered advice nor gave her opinion. Sandy would go to bed, and my mother-in-law and I would sit in the dining room every night and talk. I'd go in the bathroom and take a shot of Meth; my mother-in-law would take her sleeping pill.

"Well, I'm going to bed," she'd say.

"Stay up a little longer. I'll fix you some coffee. Then we'll talk a little; then you can go to bed."

"OK, but just a little while!" she'd answer.

We'd stay up for hours, talking about life, about philosophy. She had her sleeping pill; unknown to her, I had my Meth. I'd do all the talking, she'd be trying to keep from dozing off. "What time is it?" she would ask. I would always lie, telling her it was hours earlier than it was. She would go to bed thinking it was midnight; it was usually three in the morning.

One day, I dropped Sandy and her mother off at Dr. Benensohn's office. As they walked away from the car, I called Sandy back. I opened the trunk and handed her a large brown paper bag, folded closed at the top.

"What's that?" she asked.

"Don't open it," I said. "Just give it to Dr. Benensohn for me."

Inside the bag were all my unused vials of Methedrine, along with syringes and needles.

Ten days later, our son Matthew was born.

Chapter 5

Six weeks after Matthew's birth, we were on a flight to Los Angeles. We occupied two seats in the center of United's coach section. Sandy was breast-feeding our infant. Throughout the flight, Sandy would squeeze my hand. We were to stay for four days at my sister's home. Sarah would be there; she was coming alone from Sacramento. Abe would be there, too; he lived with my sister, Sylvia, my new brother-in-law, Max, and my thirteen-year-old nephew, Barry.

"It's strange," I thought. "The last time Sarah saw me was when I was six weeks old.

Now, she'll be meeting her new grandson, and he's six weeks old."

It was a long flight, and I had plenty of time for reflection. As we flew over mountain ranges, I remembered my days in the Air Force. At the start of my first thirty day furlough, when I was stationed at McCord AFB in Tacoma, Washington, I'd hitched a ride on an Air Force plane back to Bowman Air Field in Louisville. It took three different flights to reach my final destination. The night flight out of Texas was bumpy; the weather was bad. There was a lot of lightning and thunder. About ten of us sat in the cargo space of the C-47. The plane would bounce way up and way down. Everyone was sick, except the pilot and copilot. There were a couple of guys who, if someone had given them a gun, probably would have shot themselves in the head just to end their misery. I had my student pilot license, which I had gotten when I was seventeen, just before joining the Air Force. I loved to fly, but this one trip had me sick, too.

There was this first lieutenant, Lt. Chapman, at McCord, who took me up several times in a T-33 jet trainer. He let me handle the controls; what a thrill that was. I would do rolls and dives, and I'd bounce around the clouds. He also took me up in the T-33 several times, when he would carry the target for the F-94 jets doing their target practice. He took me up in an F-94, too. I sat in the rear, where the radar officer usually flew. He was really nice, and he encouraged me to finish college and become a pilot. Then one day, Lt. Chapman was killed. His plane crashed into the Pacific while on a night scramble mission in bad weather. He was twenty-seven.

It's amazing how people can recall events in their lives, how memory can skip around from time to time.

When I was just eighteen, I joined the Air Force. The year was 1950, during the Korean War. It wasn't that I was patriotic, it was just that I wanted to get away, to be on my own. My parents wanted to come to the train station to see me off. "Don't come," I told them. "It would be embarrassing." Besides, there was a girl I had dated who would be there. She was pretty, a student nurse. As hard as I tried, I couldn't get into her pants. She cried as I boarded the train. "Damn it," I thought. "One more night, and I know she would fuck."

There were several private coach cars attached to the train going to San Antonio, Texas. I was with a lot of others who had also enlisted. We stayed up all night, drinking and playing poker. This is fun, I thought.

The fun was short-lived. A day and a half later, we were herded off the train like cattle by uniformed airmen, who minced no words. In a drunken stupor, we all stood at attention. We were loaded into waiting buses, and off we drove to Lackland AFB for six weeks of basic training.

The stars at night are big and bright in Texas, just like the song says. Those fucking cots in those fucking tents, and those fucking frigid nights. This was bullshit. I still remember the cadence marches: "Your left, your right, you had a good home but you left, you're right!" That goddamn drill instructor; everyone wanted a poke at his fucking ugly face. I know basic training in the Air Force was supposed to be kid's stuff next to boot camp in the Marine Corps, but this was still bullshit. I don't remember ever having a hard-on in basic training; those stories about everyone being fed softpeter must have been true.

After basic training, I was transferred to Wichita Falls, Texas, for a short time. I got my first one-day pass in Wichita Falls. We all headed for the nearest whorehouse. We stood in line, like you would at a movie theater. We all had our rubbers. Finally, I was in a room with one of the many broads.

"Where you come from, airman?" she asked.

"Kentucky."

"What do you want, a fuck or a blow job?"

"Both," I answered.

She laughed, "You can't have both."

I paid ten dollars and got fucked-wham, bam, thank you sir. I swore I would never pay for it again. On my next pass, I went to a nearby airfield and rented a Piper Cub. I soloed over the open prairies for close to an hour. It was much more satisfying.

The stewardess leaned forward, offering us lunch. "I just want a soft drink," I said. Sandy ordered coffee. We pulled our tray tables down, and I held Matthew. We finished our drinks and I handed Matthew back to Sandy. He was hungry again. We let our seats recline; I closed my eyes and resumed my reminiscing.

I had driven my 1947 Chevrolet back to Washington after my furlough, passing through Chicago to see my Wicker Park family. My cousin Shirley took me to lunch at the fancy Fritzel's Restaurant on State Street in downtown Chicago. I had never been there before; it was nice. The next morning, I started my trip. I took the northern route; driving ten hours a day, it took five days. The only places I remember were Minneapolis, Minnesota, and Billings, Montana.

Minneapolis had a huge skid row section. I stopped at a night spot on its fringes. I remember one act, this guy in a tux and top hat on one side of his body, and a skimpy gown and one high-heeled shoe on the other. He would caress the side that was dressed in the gown, and the female half would caress the male side. The music, the lighting effects, the movement and contortion of masculine and feminine arms and legs made the act very erotic. I slept alone that night in some small hotel.

Billings was a nice small town. I went to a night spot. I met a girl. We drank and danced. I slept alone that night, too.

When I was eleven, I would beat my meat. I had heard that, if you beat your meat, white jazz would come out. One afternoon, when I was eleven and a half, I was beating my meat, sitting on the toilet in our apartment above the five-and-ten-cent store. All of a sudden this incredible sensation began in my cock. The feeling was a new experience for me, and then this pure white jazz erupted and shot up in the air and fell on my stomach.

Unbelievable! I rushed out of the apartment to share this great news with my best friend, Mitchell, who lived three houses down on Walnut Street; I ran up his stairs and banged on his door.

"Mitch, Mitch, open the door!" Mitchell opened the door. "What's up?"

"You're not going to believe what the fuck happened!"

"What?"

I looked around to make sure no one could hear. "I came," I said.

"You what?"

"I came...I jacked off!"

"Where?"

"At home."

"How?"

"I don't know, I've been trying for weeks, and finally, I came!"

We went into his bathroom and locked the door. I pulled down my pants and showed him my hard-on. He pulled down his pants and showed me his.

I masturbated again, and came. He masturbated, and came.

"Wow!" we echoed.

I used to jack off so much, I got an Indian rub. I had to stop, to let the skin on my penis heal.

A few months before my first masturbation, I'd fallen in puppy love. It was at Camp Tall Trees. Her name was Annette. I couldn't sleep at night. I always thought of her. It wasn't sexual; it was love. She was one month older than I and we were in the same grade at George W. Morris Grammar School. She was an A student; I was a C. After camp, her mother would bring her by our apartment. Her mother became friendly with my mother. This friendship developed after my first masturbation.

Annette's mother and my mother would sit on folding chairs outside our door on Walnut Street; it was very hot in Louisville during the month of August. Annette and I would go upstairs to play. She wore a tight sweater; she had big tits. She was the first girl I ever kissed; I was the first boy she ever kissed. We would play movie stars, experimenting with different styles of kissing. She and her mother would come over every night. After a while, I would move my hand onto her breast; she would push it off. I couldn't get past first base with her, beyond kissing. One evening, I got her on my parents' bed. I started to dry fuck her; I had her pinned. She got angry and ran downstairs. A week passed before she came over again.

"I told my mother," she said.

God, was I embarrassed!

When I turned eighteen, I was given the phone number of a girl named Ann; she was twenty-two. All my friends had laid her; she was an easy make. I called her up, and we went out. She was pretty, she was smart, she was fun. I took her to a small cheap hotel off Market Street. We undressed and got in bed. I kissed and tongued her mouth, I kissed and licked her breasts; I licked her toes, the bottoms of her feet I licked her armpits, I licked her ass. I put my head between her legs and tongued and licked her clitoris. She went wild, wild, wild. She trembled and screamed; she had an orgasm. She hugged me and cried; it was her first climax.

A week passed. I saw my friends.

"We heard you ate Ann's pussy," they said. God, was I embarrassed!

Sandy squeezed my hand. I opened my eyes. "Are you okay?" she asked.

"Yes," I smiled.

I closed my eyes and brought forth my past.

I thought about Tacoma, Seattle, Chicago and Louisville...about the girls I had known.

I thought about Frankfurt, Germany, about the Schatz I'd known.

I thought about Paris and Megeve, France, about the girls I'd known. I thought about England and Sweden, about the girls I'd known.

I thought about Paris again, about the girl I'd been engaged to. With those thoughts, I dozed off.

"This is your captain," the voice from the intercom said. "We will be landing at LAX in about twenty minutes. The skies are clear; the temperature in L.A. is seventy eight degrees. Please raise your seat backs and obey the no-smoking and seat belt lights when they appear. Remain seated until we come to a complete stop at the terminal. Thank you for flying United."

65

Sandy and I adjusted our seats. The plane shook a little as we descended. The sound of the engines increased, and we were on our final approach. A steep bank to the left, and I got a glimpse of the city, with its traffic and green hills. Soon we were at the gate and the engines were turned off. It was one o'clock, L.A. time. We watched everyone stand to disembark. When the aisle was clear, we stood up. I retrieved one small suitcase from above; we had checked a large one through. Sandy was in front of me, carrying our son. We entered the gate area.

A voice from behind the rail cried out, "Sherwin, Sandy...over here." It was my sister Sylvia, waving. A man darted forward and extended his hand.

"Hello, son."

I shook his hand. "Hello, Abe," I said. Sandy kissed him. Sylvia ran into my arms, and we kissed and hugged. Sandy and Sylvia kissed and hugged.

"This is Max," Sylvia said, as Max and I shook hands, and then Sandy and Max kissed. "This is your nephew, Barry." Sylvia smiled proudly.

I put my arm around his shoulder; I shook his hand. "Hi, Barry," I said. Sylvia kissed our son, saying, "He's so cute!" Sandy kissed and hugged Barry. I looked around; there was no one else there.

"Where's Sarah?" I asked.

"Over there," Sylvia motioned with her head.

Leaning by the rail with her back to me, about thirty feet ahead, was a woman with red hair. She had a fur stole over her shoulders. I walked toward her. I stopped, put my hand on her shoulder and squeezed softly.

"Everything's all right now," I said.

She turned, and I kissed her gently on the cheek.

Sandy approached. I took Matthew from her arms. "This is Sandy." They kissed, and Sandy introduced Matthew.

66

Sarah smiled. "He's so beautiful," she said, her eyes moist

We walked toward the main terminal. Sandy, Sarah, Sylvia and Abe were in front; Max, Barry, Matthew and I followed behind. Max made small talk about the flight, the weather, Chicago. We picked up our suitcase.

They had come in two cars. Barry sat in the rear next to Sandy, Matthew and me; Sylvia turned to face us as Max drove. Abe and Sarah followed behind us. The palm trees at the airport were nice; the weather was nice. I liked L.A.

"Where's Sarah's husband, Johnny?" I asked.

"He stayed in Sacramento. He felt Sarah should meet you alone," Sylvia answered, "Wait 'til you meet him, next time. Everyone in the family loves him."

"How long have they been married?"

"Almost ten years."

"That's right, you wrote me that. Where did they meet?" I asked.

"Gardena," Sylvia answered, smiling.

"What's that?"

"A small town that has gambling casinos. Sarah likes to play poker." She laughed.

I talked to Barry, asking him about baseball and what was happening in his life. He wanted to show me his baseball card collection when we got home.

"Did you bring your bathing suits?" Sylvia asked.

"You told us to, so we did," I replied.

No one was at a loss for words. I felt very comfortable around them. As we drove through the San Fernando Valley, I looked left and right, and was impressed with the beauty of the mountains on both sides. I could live here very easily, I thought.

It was about a forty-minute ride. We pulled into the driveway, Abe and Sarah right behind us.

"Is Sarah staying here?" I wanted to know.

"Yes," Sylvia answered.

Sylvia and Max had a two-story, four-bedroom home with a pool. It was really nice. I liked the way it was furnished. Sandy and I felt right at home. Sylvia showed us around and took us to our room. A crib had been put in our room, so we put our sleeping Matthew in it, and I helped Sandy unpack.

We went across the hall to where Sarah was staying, which was Sylvia's study and work area. Pictures covered the desk and walls. Sylvia had long blonde hair when she was in her early twenties; she was a knockout. She had already written several books, and she free-lanced for Reader's Digest and other magazines. Sandy and I walked through the living room and breakfast room. There were family pictures on the walls, faces we didn't know.

Sylvia showed us to the back yard where Sarah, Abe, Max and Barry were sitting by the pool. Several tables were set with floral centerpieces. "I'm going to be serving a late lunch soon," Sylvia said, "and a few of your relatives will be coming over. Then, tomorrow night, we will be going to one of your cousins' homes in Brentwood, and the whole family will be there, including your grandmother."

"Fine," I said, sitting down next to Sarah. "Hi," I said.

"Hi," she answered.

I really had a difficult time not staring; every chance I had, I glanced her way.

Sandy sat down and talked with Sarah. I got up and went over to sit by Abe, Max and Barry.

"So, how do you think you like California?" Abe asked.

"It looks very nice, just like they say," I replied.

I kept glancing over toward Sarah. I watched her movements, her facial expressions.

I studied her face, her body. "That's my real mother," I thought. It felt so strange.

Sylvia brought out coffee and soft drinks. "We'll eat in about an hour," she announced. She sat down next to Sarah and Sandy.

Barry brought out his baseball card collection. He really knew the game everyone's batting average and everything about baseball. I wasn't a big baseball fan. The only one I knew a little about was Stan Hack, third baseman for the Chicago Cubs years ago. I'd gotten his autograph when I was a kid. Louisville had a minor league team, the Louisville Colonels. I used to go to the games, but I was never a fan. Max was the coach for Barry's Little League team; I could tell he was a really good father.

I glanced over toward the table where Sarah had been sitting; she wasn't there. I walked over and asked Sylvia and Sandy where Sarah was. "She's in the kitchen, fixing some vegetables," Sylvia said.

I walked into the kitchen, where Sarah was bent over the sink, the water running over a bowl of vegetables. I slowly walked over to her and put my hands around her waist. She didn't move. I placed my hands on her shoulders and turned her body to face me. I looked into her eyes. I kissed her cheek close to her lips; my eyes were teary. I hugged her tightly, buried my head in her shoulder, and bawled like a baby. I couldn't hold back the tears; I just let them flow. I cried and cried and cried. She hugged me tight, she caressed my hair, she caressed my face, she kissed my face and she chokingly said, "Sherwin, Sherwin, Sherwin." She cried, too. We embraced for what seemed an eternity. Never, ever had I felt like this. All time had stopped; all that existed in this world was this moment between Sarah and me.

I eventually composed myself and gently gripped her shoulders. I looked into her eyes; they were still teary. I kissed her eyes, I kissed her cheeks, I gave her one last hug. I smiled,

"I'd better go outside." She nodded approval, she smiled. I wiped away my tears and went back outside.

I sat next to Sandy and Sylvia. "Well, you were gone quite a while," Sylvia smiled. "Yeah, I guess I was."

Sandy squeezed my hand.

More people arrived, Sylvia escorting them to the back yard and making the introductions. There were hugs and kisses all around as we met my aunts, uncles and cousins.

Sylvia appeared again, this time holding hands with a stunningly beautiful redhead. "Sherwin, this is Sarah's sister, Anne." My Aunt Anne held my hands and looked me in the face, her eyes wet. She gave me a big kiss on the mouth. She then introduced me to her husband, Irving. I also met my Aunt Mona, Sarah's youngest sister, and her husband Jerry.

I couldn't remember everyone's name, and I knew this was just a part of the family I was to meet. Sandy brought Matthew out, and everyone gathered around, smiling.

Everyone was helping themselves to food from the buffet. I sat next to Sarah.

Sandy brought me a full plate; I just nibbled, I wasn't hungry. The hours passed, the sun had set. There were kisses good-bye, more handshakes. I would see everyone again tomorrow.

Sarah was sitting, alone, on the couch in the living room. I lay down and put my head on her lap. I held her hand.

"So, tell me," she began, "were you happy growing up? Was your family nice?"

"Oh, yes, everyone was nice. I had two cousins I grew up with; they were like my sisters."

Sylvia, Sandy and Max entered the living room and sat down. "Mom, tell Sherwin what you used to do when he lived in Wicker Park," Sylvia said, smiling at me.

I looked at Sarah questioningly. She hesitated and then told me, "I would hide behind the bushes in Wicker Park and watch you walk to school with your cousin."

"Wow, and I never saw you!"

"I know," she said sadly.

"When I was older," Sylvia said, "I tried to find you, but you had moved away from Wicker Park, and I couldn't locate you. I didn't know your family had moved to Louisville."

"You know, I was a lonely kid, growing up in Louisville," I told them. "And when I was older, I always had the feeling that I was adopted. I even told Sandy a story when I first met her, how, when I was in the Air Force, stationed in Tacoma, one day I went to Seattle. I looked up my mother's name in the phone book. She's in Louisville, Kentucky, and I'm looking for her name in the Seattle phone book-like my real mother is in Seattle. Isn't that silly?"

"When were you in Seattle?" Sarah asked.

"The early fifties," I answered.

"I lived in Seattle in the early fifties," she said. We all sat in silence.

Max, Abe and Barry went to bed, and Sylvia came into our bedroom. She was wearing her nightgown and robe. I had changed into pajamas. Sandy was nursing Matthew.

"So, what did you think of the family?" She directed her question to both of us.

"Oh, they were all really nice," Sandy said.

"Who haven't we met yet?" I asked.

"Let's see, well, there's several cousins, and tomorrow, you'll meet Bubbe, your grandmother. Everybody will be there, and just wait until you see your cousin Rita's home in Brentwood! It's really gorgeous."

"Which one is Rita?" I asked.

"She's Aunt Bertha's daughter."

"And who was that real attractive redhead?"

"Oh, you mean Aunt Anne."

"That's right, Aunt Anne, and her husband is Irving," I remembered. "How many kids do they have?"

"None. I lived with them for a while when I was growing up. But I didn't stay there very long, because I was incorrigible, and they couldn't handle me," Sylvia laughed. "In fact, if you hadn't been given away for adoption, that's who you would have lived with. They talked about that many times. You would have loved living with them."

"Why?"

"They have a beautiful home in Pacific Palisades. Their next-door neighbor is the movie actor Robert Taylor. They're godparents to the Taylors' child, and you might have grown up in style."

"That's all right. I liked living above a five-and-ten-cent store in Louisville." I laughed. "Sylvia, I'm confused..."

"What, dear brother?" Sylvia smiled.

"I thought nobody had any money, and that's why I was given up for adoption." "That's true. Nobody had money in Chicago. They all moved to California. Aunt Anne met Irving in L.A.; he became very wealthy from real estate. The others opened a small bakery in L.A. The husband of one of the aunts was an out-of-work plumber, so they hired him to mix the dough. One day, he screwed up the ingredients for a coffee cake, and it came out flat and gooey. Times were tough, they had little money, so they put the gooey cake in the case for sale at half price. People started coming back and asking for the gooey coffee cake." Sylvia laughed. We all laughed. "Their company, Baker Boy, became very big all over California, even in South America. They were like Sara Lee, in California. They eventually sold the company for an awful lot of money."

"That's hysterical! What else should I know?"

"Well...Let's see...Oh, yes! You have a very famous cousin. He's Sarah's first cousin, Buck Ram."

"Buck Ram? Why is that name familiar?" I asked.

"He's a famous songwriter," Sandy volunteered.

"Yes," Sylvia agreed. "He wrote 'I'll Be Home For Christmas', 'I'm Sorry', 'You'll Never Know', 'These Precious Moments' and lots of others, plus, he discovered Ella Fitzgerald at the Apollo Theater."

"Is he going to be at Rita's tomorrow?"

"No. We hardly see him any more; he lives in Nevada. He has two daughters, one named Melody."

"That's a clever name," I remarked.

"So, Sherwin, tell me about you. What famous people were in your life?"

"Hmmm, let's see...I know!"

"Who, who, dear brother?"

"My grandfather. He died before I was born, but he was a famous Orthodox rabbi. In fact, they have his books in the Hebrew Theological College in Skokie."

"Very good, what else?"

"I know...Victor Mature."

"Victor Mature?"

"Yeah, Victor Mature. He grew up in Louisville, but he was already famous when I moved there. I used to hear stories about him; I don't know if they're true or not. I heard that he hung out at Preston and Walnut, where I lived, and that he was a troublemaker when he was a teenager. He used to steal cakes from Brown's Bakery, and meat from Fuchs' Kosher Meat Market, which was around the corner."

"Very good. What else, Sherwin?"

I thought. "I know," I said, excitedly, "I haven't even told Sandy this story; I had forgotten all about it."

"What story?" they said in unison.

"My mother's best friend is Reba Pesmen. Her husband's name is Lou, and they have two sons, Hal, short for Harold, and Al. They had a summer cottage right on the beach of Lake

Michigan, in the Indiana Sand Dunes. Every summer my mother and I would take the train and spend a week there. Lou was a commercial artist, working for the Kraft Cheese Company off Michigan Boulevard in Chicago."

"Sherwin, get to the point," Sandy said.

"Okay. Many, many years ago, before I was born, my mother lived in Kansas City, Missouri, and so did Reba and Lou Pesmen. Lou had his own commercial art studio, and he had a lot of artists working for him. One day he called this young artist into his office, and said, "Son, business has been bad, and I'm going to have to let you go, but before I do, let me give you a word of advice. You'll never get anywhere drawing those mice."

Sandy and Sylvia stared at me. "You're not going to say what we think you're going to say, are you?"

"Yes, I am. Lou Pesmen fired Walt Disney!"

"Sherwin, are you telling the truth?" Sandy asked.

"Sure. When we get back to Chicago, I'll show you a picture my mother has of Walt Disney and Lou, taken years later, after Disney became famous. The picture is signed by Disney, and it says 'To Lou Pesmen, my first boss in the art world'."

"That's a funny story," Sylvia laughed. "Listen, I'm going to bed. I'm very tired." She kissed Sandy and Matthew and gave me a big hug and kiss, saying, "Good night, dear brother."

Sarah stood by our bedroom door. She wore her nightgown and robe. "I'm going to bed," she said.

"Come on, sit down and talk to us for a while," I invited.

"OK, just for a little while."

I patted the bed and raised the pillow against the headboard. "Sit down here." I put my head on her lap and held her hand. It was very cozy. Sandy was still breast-feeding Matthew. There we were, the four of us in bed. "Did you used to sing 'Yiddishe Momme' on the Jewish Hour radio program?" I asked her.

"Yes, how did you know?"

"Well, Sylvia wrote that you used to sing on the program," I told her. "What years did you sing on the radio?"

"Hmm, let me think...I sang on the radio just after you were born. I stopped for several years. Uh, you must have been about five when I started singing again."

"When I lived in Wicker Park, everyone used to listen to the Jewish Hour. I remember this female voice singing 'Yiddishe Momme'...was that you?" I asked quietly.

"It could have been. I used to sing on radio station WOES from the Guyon Paradise Ballroom on Friday nights."

"Sing it for us now," I asked her.

"No." She smiled coyly.

"Why?"

"I can't sing any more."

"You can, too!"

"No, no, I can't," she smiled.

"Okay, I'll let you off the hook, on one condition."

"What's that?"

"Hum just one short bar."

She hummed the melody.

"Yep, that was you," I said softly. We all laughed.

Sandy moved Matthew to her other breast. "Did you breast-feed me when I was born?"

"For a short time."

"Why did you give me away for adoption?"

"Because Abe and I were going to get a divorce, and we didn't have any money to give you a good home."

"Was Abe the father?"

Sandy kicked me. "Sandy, stop kicking me."

"Of course Abe was the father," Sarah replied.

"Did he think he wasn't the father?" I had to ask.

"Of course he knew he was the father! You sure ask a lot of questions, but go ahead, ask whatever you want. But I'm going to sleep now, we'll talk tomorrow." She kissed the three of us good night and crossed the hall to her room.

I was up early the next morning. I put on my bathing suit, grabbed a towel, and went out by the pool. Abe was sitting on the patio, reading the paper, smoking a cigarette and drinking coffee.

"Hi, Abe."

"Good morning, Sherwin."

"I'm going to take a quick swim and then I'll join you."

"Good."

I dove into the water, swam several laps, and then climbed up the pool ladder. I was invigorated. I dried off, walked over to Abe, spread the towel over the deck chair and sat down.

"Want some coffee?"

"Sure," I said. I looked at the cigarette Abe was smoking; I noticed the beige cigarette case with several filterless cigarettes inside. Next to the case were empty cigarette papers, a metal roller and a screwdriver-type device.

"Can I try one of those cigarettes?"

"Sure, Sherwin."

I watched him spread the tobacco evenly onto the roller. He closed the roller and put an empty cigarette paper on the tip of the roller. With the screwdriver-like instrument, he pushed the tobacco from one end into the paper at the other end, using his chest to push the instrument as both of his hands steadied the newly formed cigarette.

With a tailor's scissors, he clipped the excess tobacco off the ends of the cigarette. "Can you do that by hand?"

"Oh, sure," Abe replied. "I always used to do it by hand, but now I mostly use the roller." He lit my cigarette.

We talked about California, and how he liked the weather. He told me he could never move back to Chicago. Except for a few close friends, he didn't miss it. I learned about his being in

76

the Polish army when he was a young man. I didn't probe; he didn't probe. We talked in generalities.

Sarah, Sylvia, Max and Barry came out by the pool. Sarah sat on a lounge chair, smoking a cigarette and watching as the rest of us swam.

Early in the afternoon, a few aunts I had already met arrived. One of the aunts was a storyteller; she had us in stitches with her jokes and the various accents to fit each situation. She should have been a professional comedian.

Later that evening, Max drove us all to Brentwood, where I was to meet still more family members. The house was in the hills, set back off a private road with a circular driveway. We entered the foyer, with its white marble floors; glancing into the living room, I saw a beautiful white grand piano. It was a California-style home, really plush.

Everyone was there. There were big hugs and kisses from my aunts, handshakes from my uncles, kisses from my female cousins, handshakes from my male cousins.

Sarah and all her sisters led Sandy, Matthew and me over to Bubbe. She sat in the formal living room, on a high-backed armchair, a blanket covering her lap. She extended her frail hand for me to hold. I sat on a footstool at her side. She asked if I knew who she was.

"Yes," I answered.

"Who?" she asked.

"You're the Queen Bee," I responded. Everyone smiled.

She studied my face, she looked into my eyes. "You looka da same," she said in her old-country English. Everyone laughed.

I was her oldest grandson. I introduced her to Sandy and her great-grandson.

That night, Sarah and Sylvia sat on our bed, both in their nightgowns. Sandy nursed our son. I laid my head on Sarah's lap. I asked about the cousins, about who belonged to whom. I had trouble keeping track. I learned that I had been named after Bubbe's husband.

The next day, all the aunts and uncles came over in the afternoon. Several of the cousins were there, too.

That evening, Max, Sylvia, Sandy and I went to the Magic Castle, a popular nightclub. It was fun; all the tables had magicians performing card tricks, coin tricks and other sleight-of-hand tricks. They also had a piano that played requests, but there was no piano player. I've always liked magic!

Sarah, Abe and Barry stayed home, with Sarah looking after Matthew. When we returned late that evening, Sylvia and Max went to bed and Sarah came into our bedroom. We talked. I asked her again, "Did Abe think he was not the father?"

"Yes," she said.

"Was he the father?"

"Yes, Abe was the father."

The next morning, Sarah told Sandy how, when they were separated, she had gone to visit Abe one afternoon. Sylvia was living with an aunt. Sarah and Abe got into an argument. Moments later they embraced and, in the heat of passion, they had sex and I was conceived. Sarah was seeing a married man at the time, but she swore to Sandy that it was Abe who was the father. The grandmother, the aunts, and the uncles all sided with Abe, and they wouldn't believe Sarah. It was many years later that they finally accepted Sarah's word that Abe was really the father.

That afternoon we were to leave for Chicago. We said good-bye to Abe and Barry.

Sarah gave me her address.

"Will you write?" she asked.

"I don't know," I told her, truthfully.

We hugged, we kissed. Sandy hugged and kissed Abe, Barry and Sarah. Max and Sylvia drove us to the airport. We said good-bye.

On the flight, I was murmuring.

"What are you doing?" asked Sandy.

"I'm counting...just a minute. Do you know how many aunts, uncles, first cousins, parents, grandparents and nephews I have between California and Chicago?"

"No, how many?"

"Sixty-nine," I said.

Sandy smiled. I closed my eyes and thought of Paris. Then I dozed off.

Chapter 6

Later in the week after we returned from California, Sandy and I had my cousins Deanie and Shirley and their husbands over to our apartment. I told them about our trip to Los Angeles. I told them about Sylvia, Sarah, Abe and the rest of the California family.

"Are you going to tell your parents?" they asked.

"No, I don't want them to know." I said. They didn't comment one way or the other.

Sunday we went to my parents' apartment for lunch. Except for Deanie and Shirley, all of the Wicker Park family were there. We had told them we had gone to California to visit some of Sandy's relatives. Everything was back to normal. The following week we received a letter from Sylvia:

August 6, 1963

Dearest Sherwin and Sandy,

I hope that you have settled down by now after the emotion packed four days you spent with us. I miss all of you already and if you got the idea that I was not as affectionate as I should have been please try to understand. Any of my friends or family (except for my parents) will tell you that I am a very warm and loving person, but I'm afraid having Sarah here just cramped my style to be perfectly honest. I felt as though she had many years to make up for as best as she could and that I had better stay in the background. But, Sherwin I truly

*love you and I couldn't have asked for a better brother
and sister-in-law if I had cut you both out from my own
pattern. I guess that I was a little worried about how you
would feel about me as part of the reason I go to a
psychiatrist is due to my lack of confidence in my ability
to hold anyone's love. I am really quite full of complexes.*

*Anyway, I hope that you feel better now little brother
and that you will go about your life happily. You have a
wonderful wife and that son of yours is the whole world.*

*Sarah said to tell you that she is sorry that she forgot
to kiss the baby good-bye in all of the excitement. Barry
sends his best and so do Max and Abe. You didn't get to
talk much to Abe, but he did want to talk to you, Sherwin,
only he told me that when he tried to he became so
nervous that he just couldn't talk sensibly. We have to put
the past behind us, all of us and live for the present and
the future. I, for one, am very happy to have my brother
again and I hope that in time we get to know one another
the way a brother and sister should know one another.*

*I am looking forward to my next therapy session as I
have so many feelings to discuss. It will take me hours to
unravel the emotions of the past week.*

*Please write soon and let me know how you feel now
that you are back in home territory. Be well and be good
to each other as Matthew needs you both very much.*

All my love, Sylvia

I enjoyed hearing from Sylvia, but I had no desire to go
back to California. My family were all in Chicago. My Wicker
Park family, Deanie and Shirley's five children. My father's
brothers-my uncles, their wives-my aunts. My father's sister,
my aunt; her daughter, my first cousin. All the other first,
second and third cousins I had. I always enjoyed seeing

everyone. This was my family. But California, that was my family too. Sylvia was my real sister; I could be kooky with Sylvia-she was kooky, too. I thought of all the pictures of me with my mother, where I would always pull away when she wanted to be close. With Sarah, it was just the opposite, I was drawn close to her. I wanted to be next to her. My aunts, uncles and cousins in California, they all seemed so nice. But I really didn't know them. My aunts, uncles and cousins in Chicago I knew; I had known them all my life. They all were part of me. I was really mixed up...I was torn between Chicago and L.A. I went to the drugstore near the apartment. I refilled my prescription for Methedrine, syringes and needles.

I didn't hide it from Sandy. She was disappointed, but we didn't argue.

The following Sunday we were sitting around the dining room table eating lunch at my parents' apartment-my mother, father, Ojeh, Onnie, Uncle Sam, Sandy and I. As we ate I casually announced, "I found out I'm adopted. When Sandy and I went to California, I met my sister. You know I have a sister, don't you?"

Sandy almost choked on her gefilte fish. My mother looked at me; she had a smile on her face. My father looked at me, awaiting my next words. Uncle Sam and Onnie looked at me. Ojeh, already a little hard of hearing, said, "You're a doctor. You got a cyst. What'd you say?"

"I said I found out I'm adopted and I went to California. I met my real sister; her name is Sylvia. I also met my natural mother and father. I also met aunts, uncles and cousins." I said everything with no emotion, very factually. "Ma, pass the horseradish, please."

We ate in silence. Everyone was waiting for me to say something. I had nothing else to say.

Later, Deanie, Shirley, their husbands and kids came over for dessert. After a while, Sandy and I got up to leave. As always, I kissed my mother and Ojeh good-bye.

"Is your sister ever going to visit you in Chicago?" my mother asked.

"One day, she plans to," I said.

"Dad and I would like you to bring her over here."

"Sure, Ma...she'd like that."

I kissed my mother good-bye again.

Driving home Sandy said, "You're too much. I thought you weren't going to tell your parents."

"I changed my mind. I'm tired of secrets. I don't like secrets; I wanted everything out in the open. Did you notice my mother's face? Did you notice my father's face? Did you notice the smiles on their faces? It was as if a big weight was removed from their bodies."

"I know," Sandy said. "Your mother told me when we were alone that she was glad you'd found out. She never wanted to tell you because she was afraid you would be hurt. They were happy for you that you found your sister. Your mom wants me to call her later to make sure you're OK."

"I'm fine," I said.

Chapter 7

The weeks and months had passed. I had stopped taking Methedrine. Everything was normal and uneventful; perhaps it was the still before the storm. Sandy and I were invited to a party one Saturday night in the fall. Our hostess introduced us to a couple.

"Jack, this is Sandy."

"Hi, Sandy."

"And this is her husband, Sherwin."

"Hi, Jack."

"Hi, Sherwin." We shook hands.

"And this is Audrey," our hostess said.

"Hi, Audrey," Sandy said.

"Very nice meeting you, Audrey." I shook her hand.

What a body, what a smile...and that long red hair. God, I wish I wasn't married, I thought.

I mingled with the crowd. Sandy and Audrey spent a lot of time together; they seemed to like each other.

Driving home, Sandy said, "Aren't Jack and Audrey really nice?"

"Yes," I said. "Are they going together?"

"No, they're just good friends. Isn't she beautiful?"

"Uh...yes, she's nice."

"We're to get together next week, and the four of us are to go out for dinner."

"Fine."

I drove the babysitter home, my mind on Audrey.

84

The following Friday night the four of us met at Agostino's, an Italian restaurant on the city's Near North Side. Sandy told the story of my adoption, and Jack and Audrey were fascinated with the tale. Audrey kept asking me questions.

She was a little teary over the story. I knew I had to see her again, alone.

The following Monday, around six in the evening, I gave myself a shot of Methedrine in the arm. I drove to the Belmont Hotel on Sheridan Road near Lake Michigan, not far from our apartment and just a block from where Audrey lived. I had looked up her number in the phone book. I stepped into the drugstore in the hotel. The night was cool, not cold. I wore a light overcoat over a corduroy shirt. I dialed.

"Hello."

"Audrey?"

"Yes."

"Sherwin," I said.

"Sherwin, hi. Where are you?" She heard the noise of the cash register nearby.

"I'm at the drugstore at the Belmont Hotel. If you're not busy, I thought I'd stop over and say hello."

"Sure," she said.

"Can I bring you coffee or a Coke?"

"Yes, I'll have a Coca-Cola."

She gave me her address and apartment number. I ordered a large black coffee and a large Coke to go from the food counter.

A block and a half and I was there. I rang the bell.

"Come on up, I'm on the second floor," her voice said from the intercom. She buzzed me in.

She opened the door. Gone was the ponytail. Her long red hair covered her shoulders. She wore tight black slacks. She filled her white blouse. No makeup; she didn't need it. Her green eyes glowed.

"Hi, Sherwin, come on in."

She had a small studio apartment. One room, a breakfast area, a bathroom. That was it. It was nice, very comfortable. Her bed was in a corner of the large room. A sofa, a coffee table, a few chairs. I felt right at home.

We sat on the sofa and had our drinks. We talked. I made her laugh. She was a secretary for an advertising agency on Michigan Boulevard. She liked her work. She was twenty-six and had been going with one of the star football players for the Chicago Bears. They had broken up three months ago. I had to use self-control not to kiss her as we talked. I touched her hand; she touched my arm.

"It's eight o'clock. I'd better go," I said.

She saw me to the door. She was five foot five. I was five foot eleven. I faced her; I held her shoulders. I gently kissed her cheeks. I gave her a soft short kiss on the lips.

"I'd like to see you again," I said. She nodded yes.

"I'll call you tomorrow night."

"OK," she said.

I left. Holy shit, I'm in love, I thought.

"Hi, hon, where have you been?" Sandy asked.

"I had some late appointments. I got stood up. This guy's wife told me to stop by tomorrow night at nine and I'll catch her husband at home. I'll be home late tomorrow," I said.

The next evening, I showered and shaved. I gave myself a pop in the ass. At six p.m., I was at the drugstore at the Belmont Hotel. I dialed the number.

"Hello."

"Hi," I said.

"Hi, where are you?"

"I'm at the drugstore. Is it OK to come over?"

"Sure."

86

"I'll be there in a few minutes."

I rang the bell.

She buzzed me in. I knocked on her apartment door. Audrey stood there. In her white slacks, black blouse and high heels, she was gorgeous. I placed the bag with the coffee and Coke on the small table by the door. I closed the door. I placed my hands around her waist. I kissed her full on the mouth. We hugged.

"God, I couldn't wait to see you," I whispered.

"Me, too," she said.

I took off my coat. We sat on the couch and embraced. We kissed passionately. I placed my hands on her shoulders. I gently pushed her back a little.

"Wow," I said, "we'd better have a drink."

"Yeah," she answered.

I stood up and got the bag. I placed her Coke and my coffee on the coffee table in front of us.

She took a sip. We talked. I held her hands and spread my fingers between her fingers. With my right hand I lightly touched her face. I lightly rubbed my fingers around her eyebrows, on her forehead. I caressed her nose with my fingers. I moved my fingers around her lips, around her cheeks and her ears. I looked into her eyes. We kissed again, a long passionate kiss. We stood up.

"I'm going to turn the lamp off," I said.

"OK."

The light from the breakfast area was on; we could see in the dim light. We stood and kissed. I unbuttoned her blouse. She unbuttoned my shirt. I took off my shirt. I undid the back of her bra. She took off her blouse and then her bra. Her breasts were big, beautiful. I lowered my head and kissed her breast above her left nipple and then I kissed her right breast above that nipple. I led her toward the bed in the corner of the room. I slipped off my shoes, took off my pants, my socks. I sat on the bed, lowering her slacks as she stood in front of me. I kissed her stomach, her belly button. I pulled down the blanket, the sheet. I laid her down on the bed. I pulled off her slacks. I pulled off my shorts. She pulled off her panties. I kissed her cheek. I kissed her ear. I licked her neck. I ran my tongue over her outstretched right arm. I licked her shoulder, her arm, her hand, her fingers. I licked her armpit. I ran my tongue down her side. I switched sides and repeated on her left what I had done on her right. I raised her foot. I licked her toes, her ankle, her thigh. I placed my head between her legs. I kissed and licked the bottom of her stomach. I kissed her breast. I licked her nipples. I turned her over on her stomach. I kissed and licked her back. I ran my tongue all over her body. I tongued her ears. There was no part of her anatomy that I did not lick and tongue. I was giving her around the world, and I loved doing it. I did this for well over an hour. I turned her over on her back. I placed my head between her legs again. I kissed her clitoris, I gently tongued her vagina. I felt for the hardness of the clitoris and I slowly tongued her spot. Her hands held my head. I enjoyed the sounds she made. I could tell how much she enjoyed what I was doing. I moved my body around. My head was facing down between her thighs. My hard cock was over her face. I could feel her hand holding my cock. She licked and kissed my hard-on; her lips and hands put my cock in her mouth. God, I loved it. I knew that if we kept this up I would come in her mouth.

I didn't want to do that, not tonight. I moved around. I rested on my knees facing her; I held my cock and rubbed it gently against her cunt. I rubbed it against her clitoris, up and down I rubbed ...very, very slowly. I kissed her lips, I French-kissed her mouth. I looked into her eyes.

"Oh, Audrey," I said.

"Oh, Sherwin," she moaned.

I placed just the head of my hard cock into her vagina. I

slowly moved just the head in and out. I refused to give her more until she asked for more. Her moans increased.

It made me all the more excited. I held back, just the head of my cock moving slowly in and out. I still wouldn't give more...not until she asked for more.

I had all the time in the world.

"Oh, Sherwin."

"What?"

"Put it in."

"Put what in?"

"Put it in."

"Put what in?"

"Sherwin."

"What?"

"Please."

"Please what?"

"Put it in."

"Put what in?"

"Put your cock in." Her sounds became louder.

"Put my cock in what?"

"Put your cock in my cunt," she screamed.

Slowly I put a little more into her vagina. "Like that?" I asked.

"More," she said.

"More what?" I asked.

"Oh, Sherwin."

"More what?" I repeated.

"Sherwin."

"Say it, Audrey. Say it, Audrey."

"Fuck me. Fuck me," she begged.

"Oh, baby," I said. I gave her a little more of my hard-on.

"Oh, oh, oh, oh!" She was having an orgasm.

I withdrew all but the head of my cock.

"Come on, baby, come on...that's it...come, come."

"Sherwin, Sherwin, Sherwin," she screamed.

She had a long hard orgasm. I slowly put more of my cock in her vagina. I slowly moved it in and out, in and out.

"Sherwin, stop. Sherwin, stop," she begged.

"No, I won't stop. I'm going to give you more of my cock. All you have to do is ask. Ask, Audrey, and I'll give you all of my cock. I'm hard, real hard. Do you want all my cock?"

"Yes."

"Say it."

"More," she pleaded.

"More what...say it, Audrey. More what?

"Oh God," she screamed, "Fuck me, fuck me."

"Say it again, Audrey. Say it again."

"Oh God, oh God, please, please fuck me, fuck me. Give me your cock...all your cock...Oh God, please fuck me! " she screamed wildly.

I gave her all my cock. She felt all my cock. She screamed, she cried. She had multiple orgasms. I came. I came big-time.

Her body was quivering, her hands were shaking, she hugged me real real tight and hard.

"Oh, God, never, never did I come like that, my God," she cried. She kissed my lips. "My God, my God. I love you. I love you."

I didn't arrive back at my apartment until after one. Sandy was sleeping. Our son was asleep in his crib.

The next morning I was up at seven. I showered, shaved and got ready for work. Sandy awakened.

"Hi, what time did you get home?" she asked.

"Real late...what time did you go to sleep?"

"About eleven."

"I probably got home a little after eleven. You were already asleep." I took a pop in the arm and went out selling.

Later that evening, when I arrived home, Sandy said,

"Sherwin, guess who's coming over for dinner Thursday night?"

"Who?"

"Audrey and maybe Jack."

"Uh."

"I called Audrey and invited her and Jack for dinner. She said she hadn't talked to Jack for a while, but she would call him. I told her to come alone if Jack can't make it."

"That's nice," I said.

Thursday evening, Audrey arrived alone. I couldn't believe this whole fucking scene. I liked Audrey. I could get serious with Audrey. Hell, I'm married, I got a kid. I just had a fling. That's all. Now my wife's inviting her over to the apartment for dinner. Holy shit, I thought. I went into the bathroom and had a pop.

I fixed Sandy and Audrey a martini; I had a club soda. We sat in the living room and talked. Later we went into the dining room. Sandy had set the table beautifully; there was candlelight, a bottle of wine...the mood was very romantic. I poured the wine into three glasses, but I didn't touch mine. I drank water instead. The meal was gourmet; Sandy's an excellent cook. Everyone was relaxed, including me. I'm always funny and witty when I do Meth. I had everyone laughing.

Later that evening, Sandy and Audrey kissed good night and I drove her home. "How come you never called?" Audrey asked.

"I don't know...I was going to."

"When?"

"Soon."

She moved closer to me as I drove. There was an empty spot in front of her building.

I parked and we sat and talked. We kissed.

"If I call in sick tomorrow, can you come over?" I looked

91

into her eyes, hesitating.

"Yes...what time?"

"Ten."

"OK, I'll see you tomorrow morning at ten."

We kissed. I drove home.

A full-blown affair developed. I was seeing Audrey four and five times a week. Sometimes I stopped over at her apartment for just a short time. We had lunch together at least once a week on Michigan Boulevard during her lunch hour. She would call Sandy often, hoping I would answer the phone. I fell in love with Audrey. December came and Sandy took Matthew to Denver to be with her parents for a few weeks during the holidays.

I stayed overnight at Audrey's while Sandy was in Denver. I told her about the Methedrine; I shot up in front of her. She never wanted to try it; she was afraid of needles. She preferred wine. I could have snapped the head off a vial and poured it into her soft drink or coffee. She would have gotten an effect, but I never did.

I would go to my apartment after work every day. I would call Sandy in Denver. I would leave Audrey's apartment every morning about six-thirty to go home and change and go to work. The whole situation was a honeymoon of sorts, but I was beginning to get bored. I was beginning to miss Sandy and Matthew. I thought about breaking off the relationship with Audrey when Sandy returned.

I knew it would be tough. One morning at my apartment, as I was about to leave for work, the phone rang.

"Hello," I said.

"Sherwin."

"Sandy...What are you doing calling so early? Is everything all right?"

"Yes...is everything alright with you?"

"Yes, why?"

"I've been calling all night...every hour on the hour. Where were you?"

"What do you mean where was I? I was here. I must have fallen asleep."

"Bullshit. Where were you?"

"I was here," I repeated.

"Bullshit. Have you been seeing Audrey?"

"What are you talking about?"

"Have you been seeing Audrey?"

I paused ...I thought. I hate secrets, I hate lies, I hate deceit. I'm such a fucking asshole.

"Yes," I said. There was a pause.

"Are you in love with her?" Sandy's voice was very controlled.

"I was...but not any more, " I said.

"Does she love you?"

"I don't know. I think so."

"What are you going to do?" Sandy's voice was still controlled. I thought for a moment.

"I know," I said.

"What?"

"Would you call her up and talk to her and break up the relationship?"

"Are you crazy?" Sandy screamed.

"Yeah, I'm crazy."

"What's Audrey's phone number?" Sandy's voice was in control again.

I gave her the number.

"Don't leave. I'll call you back after I talk to her."

I waited by the phone. Ten minutes...twenty minutes...thirty minutes. The phone rang.

"Hello," I said.

"Sherwin."

"Yes."

"I had a long talk with Audrey...She is in love with you. She felt very bad because of me...and she's not going to see you any more."

I sighed in relief, "Ah, great. Thanks. When are you coming home?"

"I'm catching the five o'clock train. I'll be home tomorrow. Pick us up at Union Station tomorrow morning at nine."

"Tomorrow. I thought you weren't coming back until next week."

"I will be there tomorrow...you pick me up." Her voice was still controlled.

"OK. Good-bye," I said.

She hung up.

I filled the syringe with the long needle with a cc of Methedrine. The phone rang.

I put the syringe down. "Hello."

"Sherwin."

"Hi, Audrey."

"What did you do? I can't believe you told Sandy about us. Are you crazy?" She was clearly upset.

"Yes, I'm crazy," I said.

"I can't believe you did that. I can't believe you told her."

"Audrey...Let's have lunch. I'll meet you in the lobby of your building at noon."

"All right...I'll see you at noon. She hung up.

I picked up the syringe. I looked at the fluid line resting on 1cc. I snapped another vial open and fed the fluid into the syringe. It rested at 2 cc. I shot myself in the ass. It was a bad aim ...it hurt. I probably deserved that, I thought.

I was on time...we walked out of the building onto Michigan Boulevard.

It was cold and windy, snowing lightly. We walked in silence around the corner to a small restaurant.

It was crowded. We were lucky; we had to wait only fifteen

minutes. The waitress brought us menus.

"I'm just going to have coffee," I said.

"That's all I want," Audrey said.

I gave the waitress our order. She looked at me.

"That's all we want is coffee. I'll take care of you with the tip." I smiled.

She shrugged. "Two coffees, OK. "

I offered Audrey a cigarette. She rarely smoked. She took the cigarette. She held my hand as I lit our cigarettes.

"I can't believe you did that, Sherwin. " She spoke softly, her voice choked. Her eyes were teary.

"Audrey, this just couldn't go on...I'm married. I got a kid. I'm sorry that I hurt you...but this had to end."

"You're a bastard," she said.

"I know...I'm really a bastard. I know I'm a bastard ...I'm sorry." I was a little choked up. I really did like her.

"I'm going. I can't stay here any more," she said.

She got up and left the table. I watched her beautiful body and long red hair sway down the aisle. As usual, all the men's heads turned to watch. She was gone. I would never see her again. God, I thought, I wish polygamy was legal. I wished Sandy, Audrey and I could live together.

"Oh well," I murmured.

I got up, left a twenty-dollar tip, and went out selling.

The next morning, I was at Union Station. The train was on time. It was really cold, and my breath blew smoke as I walked beside the train that had just pulled in and come to a noisy halt. The steam from the engine filled the walkway as I looked for Sandy's coach. There she was, the porter helping her down the steps. She was holding Matthew; he was just about seven months old. The porter placed her two suitcases by her side. I waved as I approached.

"Hi," I said. I started to kiss her, but she moved her head

away. I kissed Matthew. I picked up the suitcases and followed her to the station. We walked in silence. She was a little bundle of anger, I could tell.

I left to get the car. Sandy held Matthew and waited in the station's pick-up area. Sandy came out. I put the suitcases in the trunk. She got into the back seat, holding Matthew. I drove off.

I felt like a fucking cab driver as I continued under the tunnel out into the streets that led to Wacker Drive. I headed towards the Outer Drive and got off at Montrose Avenue, and soon we were home. She waited for me to open the back door of the car. Now I felt like a fucking chauffeur. We hadn't spoken a word. I got the suitcases from the trunk and we entered our home sweet home.

She unbundled Matthew and put him in the crib. She gave him a bottle of milk.

"Aren't you breast-feeding?" I asked.

"I'm all dried up," she answered.

I really felt bad. I didn't ask why ...I knew.

"I'm going out selling. I'll see you later," I said.

She came to the door. She struck out. Her fists pounded my chest. "You bastard, you bastard. I hate you. I hate you!" she screamed. I grabbed her hands. I held them down.

"Hey, cool it," I said. "That thing between Audrey and me is over. It's over. I'll call you later. Now cool down or I ain't coming back. I'll talk to you later."

I left. I was in no mood for being a fucking insurance salesman. I went to my office. Marshall and the three girls were working. I told everyone I didn't want any calls. I closed the door of my private office. I put my feet on the desk and closed my eyes. I felt like shit.

It was six o'clock. I called Sandy. "Hi," I said.

"Hi. " She sounded mellow.

"Do you want me to pick up some Chinese food?" I asked.

"Sure."

96

"I'll see you in about an hour."

"OK."

I called ahead to the restaurant near our apartment

I brought home the food including wonton soup. We ate in silence. I didn't ask any questions. That night I fell asleep on the bed in Matthew's room. We slept in separate rooms for the next several nights.

It was New Year's Eve, but we had made no plans. I brought home a bottle of champagne. We watched television. We picked the channel that showed State Street, that Great Street in downtown Chicago. The huge crowd prepared for the countdown to midnight. I poured two glasses of champagne. I reached out my hand for Sandy to stand up. She held my hand and stood up from the couch. We each held a glass.

"You can't drink," she said.

"It's OK. I haven't had any Meth since you've been back."

"Yes, but it's still in your system."

"It's OK, I'll just have one glass."

The announcer counted down.

"10-9-8-7-6-5-4-3-2-1. Happy New Year, Happy New Year!" he hollered.

I took a sip. Sandy took a sip. I put our glasses down. I put my hands on her waist. I looked down into her hazel eyes.

"Happy New Year," I said.

She looked into my eyes. "Happy New Year...you big baboon," she smiled. We kissed.

"I love you," I said.

"I love you too." She put her arms around me. We kissed again and again and again. Her eyes were filled with tears. We hugged. We finished our drinks. I refilled her glass. We went into the bedroom and lay in each other's arms.

"How did you know I was having an affair with Audrey?" I asked.

"Sherwin, you're slurring your words."

97

"I am not, I just had one glass."

"You kook. I'm telling you, you're slurring your words. You're drunk."

"Im-pos-sible," I said. Sandy laughed. "So te-e-ll me. How did you know?"

"Oh, I suppose when she came over for dinner. I could tell the way she looked at you, the way she would laugh at what you would say. She called here a lot to talk to me, but I always felt she really wanted to talk to you."

"But...but...how did you know?"

"I didn't really know. But I had called you several nights...you were never there. And that night. I called you every hour...then I just knew. Maybe I have ESP." She laughed.

"Yep, you're my little ESP gi-r-r-l." I kissed her again, and then I fell asleep in her arms.

Chapter 8

In the days, weeks and months that followed, I read an awful lot. I had stacks of books about philosophy, books about psychology, I became totally immersed in reading about the nature of man and the human mind. I would take a pop and read until the wee hours of the morning, alone in the dining room, lying on the brown-covered daybed.

Sandy would sleep, and the next day we would discuss what I had read. I was giving myself the education that I'd never had. I found myself disagreeing with much of the thinking of the world's greats. I found myself questioning the English translation of many of the books; I felt the true meanings of the authors had been lost. I wasn't just reading; I was studying the books. I hardly ate, I hardly slept...my whole life after work was reading.

One night when the hour was late, around two and Sandy was asleep in the bedroom, I was drawn to look up from my book. I looked past the kitchen and into the breakfast room. The top half panel of the window reflected a planter that was attached to the kitchen wall; I could see the vines of the miniature plastic ivy cascading out of the loose-weave natural wicker half-basket.

I started to read again; I was almost finished with Carl Jung's autobiography, Memories, Dreams, Reflections. Again I was drawn to look at the reflection of the planter. A strange feeling engulfed my body as I gazed at the window panel. I wasn't seeing the reflection of the planter. No, I was seeing some other object in the wicker basket. I couldn't make out what it was. I walked into the kitchen and looked at the wall on my right. I saw the basket with its sprays of miniature plastic ivy and trailing green vines. I looked toward the window in the breakfast room and I saw the reflection of the planter. Strange, my eyes are playing tricks on me, I thought. I lay back down on the daybed and continued to read. After a few minutes, I turned my head toward the window again. My God, I thought, what in the world is that? I looked, but still I did not get up. Goose bumps rose as I stared. I was still. My God, I thought, I think I'm seeing my soul. I closed my eyes, hoping it would go away. I had just read something about the soul. I closed the book. I opened it to a page at random.

I don't believe this, I thought. There it was on the page. Carl Jung had written about the soul. I looked again toward the window. The strange reflected object was still there. This is silly; this can't be, I thought. I closed the book and then I randomly reopened it to another page. There was more about the soul. I looked at the window. I was almost afraid to walk into the kitchen to see the planter, but I went. The planter was there, the reflection from the window showing it as I stood in the kitchen.

I returned to the daybed. Again, I saw not the planter reflected but the object; it was almost as if it was a head of sorts. I became used to the sight of it. It was like a game I was playing. I closed my eyes. I slowly opened one as if to catch the object off guard. I couldn't; it was still there. I got up and went into the kitchen. I studied the planter. I shivered slightly. I studied the window. The still of the night, a feeling of cat and mouse. I lay back on the daybed.

"Holy shit," I softly murmured. "What is that?" I looked at the window. The object was gone; the reflection of the planter was gone. What I saw was unbelievable. It wasn't scary at all-it was a picture, as if a slide had been projected onto the window.

My God, I thought again, what is that?

I saw a picture of a man standing motionless on a street paved with squares of stone. He wore the attire of long, long ago-a skirt above the knees, sandals with strange straps wrapping partway up his legs. What is this? I thought again and again. I walked into the kitchen; I looked at the breakfast window-the picture was still there. I could see it very clearly, very detailed, just as I could see from the daybed. I walked into the breakfast room. I stood and looked right in front of the upper panels of the window. I could still see the man, the scene-- but not as clearly. I had to stand in the kitchen or by the daybed to focus for its clarity.

I still was not afraid. I found this to be astonishing. Who is that person, I asked myself. He looked to be in his early twenties; clean-shaven with no bodily hair, except for his head, where the hair was black, full and kind of long. Is that me? I wondered.

Yes...it is me. No...that's not me; he looks kind of like me, but maybe it's not me. I looked hard again. I stood in the kitchen. My God, I thought, I think that's Sandy. Yes, that's Sandy. No...wait a minute...it's me. No, it's... it's... it's Sandy and me. My God, I am seeing her or me, I couldn't tell which. I was seeing my past life. No. I was seeing Sandy's past life. My God, my God...Sandy is my soul mate. I thought that the picture was the anima Carl Jung had written about. I hurried back to the daybed and picked up the book, randomly choosing a page. Carl Jung was explaining the anima.

This was incredible. The experience was a treasure. I asked myself questions about the anima, about the soul. After each question, I randomly opened a page of the book. The answer to my question was there. I recalled other things Jung had written. I was able to instantly turn to that page of the book. I kept closing and opening the book at random. I was amazed at my ability to turn to the page of a subject I wanted. It was uncanny.

I stared at the white wall in the dining room, I closed my eyes, I lay on my back. Suddenly, I felt a force, the pull of it drawing me through a long black tunnel. I started to spin. I saw flashes of light. It frightened me, and I forced my eyes open. I was afraid to close them again. I feared being drawn through this tunnel. I was afraid of the feeling of the spin, of the unknown.

I forced myself to sit up. The picture of me, Sandy or both of us was still "projected" on the window. When I turned off the light in the kitchen, the scene on the window was gone, and it reappeared when I turned the light back on. I figured that for some strange reason, I had activated a memory cell, one from centuries ago. I had materialized that memory from that cell and projected it onto the window. It made sense to me. It explained the picture on the window, the object, the soul, the planter. I could not figure out how it had happened. The force that had tried to draw me down and through the tunnel to another end, perhaps another place, I could not understand ...it scared me. I was afraid to give up my will and let the force pull me through the tunnel.

I stayed up; I couldn't sleep. And when the dawn appeared, I could still see the picture on the window. It was still clear; it was real. As it became lighter outside the picture faded and then was gone.

I couldn't wait to tell Sandy about my experience. I knew I could never tell anyone else. It was too incredible; no one would believe it. I wouldn't believe it if someone told me. I would say they were hallucinating from the Methedrine. But Sandy, I could tell her anything. Sandy, I knew, would believe me. Hurry up, Sandy, wake up, I thought. I showered and shaved. I gave myself a shot of Methedrine. I needed it to get me through the day since I'd had no sleep. Sandy would awaken soon. I would tell her about my experience. I would go out selling. I would come home early and get some sleep, and then tonight, who knew what tonight might bring?

Chapter 9

As I was driving home later that day, I thought about all that had happened.

Is it possible, I thought, that Carl Jung's research into the anima and the animus was brought to life? Is it possible that Carl Jung died without having discovered the human potential of being capable of projecting one's anima onto glass? Does glass contain a substance that allows the projection of one's memory to be seen by all? Jung's definition of anima referred to the female characteristics of all males. His definition of animus referred to the male characteristics of all females. Was *his* decision to leave *as* "riddles" or "mysteries" certain "inexplicable" elements that some would claim to be in the realm of the psychic a result of fear of rejection by the scientific community? How does one duplicate a paranormal experience at will? I certainly couldn't; it had happened just that one time. I didn't consciously make it happen. It just happened. To me, a vision is something of a very personal nature: one has a vision; nobody else, or perhaps a select few, sees that vision. My experience was not a vision. Anyone who had been there would have seen the picture on the window.

I stopped at a camera store on the way home. I bought a Polaroid camera and film. I could hardly wait until it became dark. If this scene from a distant past reappeared on the breakfast window, I would not only have Sandy *as* a witness, I would have a picture. At home I showed Sandy the camera and film. I told her I was going to sleep for a few hours and that later we would stay up together to see if the picture of her or me from centuries ago would reappear. Sandy seemed very concerned about me. She wanted to believe, but any rational mind would not accept the reality of my description. She hoped that perhaps this was a miracle of sorts...after all, I was her husband ... hopefully, her sane husband.

I set the alarm to give myself about four hours of sleep. I got up, showered, shaved, brushed my teeth, and gave myself a pop in the ass. It was ten p.m. Sandy and I sat on the daybed in the dining room. I had the loaded Polaroid by my side. We looked past the kitchen and into the window in the breakfast room. The dining room light was on, the kitchen light was on, the breakfast room light was off. Everything was as it had been the previous night. The planter on the kitchen wall was reflected in the top panel of the breakfast room window. Everything was normal. Sandy and I awaited the unknown.

Sandy was reading a novel; I just sat

Several hours passed. Sandy looked up from her book. "Sherwin, I'm getting tired...I think I'll go to bed."

"Do you want some Meth?" I asked.

"No. I do not want Meth."

Sandy stood up. "I'm going to fix some coffee. Do you want some?"

"No. I'll take a soft drink."

A few minutes later, Sandy called out. "Sherwin, come in the breakfast room. Let's drink here."

She had turned on the light in the breakfast room. I got up, carrying my Polaroid. I laid the camera down on the table, and we sipped our drinks and smoked our cigarettes. I stood by the window; outside was the back yard, and across it was the back of a three story apartment building on the next street Beyond was the tall apartment building on Marine Drive. There were no lights on in the three-story building. The tall apartment complex showed the lights from various apartments. I reached for the Polaroid and took a picture of the window.

"What are you doing?" Sandy asked.

"I just wanted to take a picture of the window."

I snapped the picture, pulled the film out of the side of the camera, and after thirty seconds, peeled off the negative. I coated the film with the stick of developer in its little plastic tube and watched as the image slowly appeared.

"Holy shit," I said.

Sandy looked up at me. "What?"

"Holy shit," I repeated.

I sat next to Sandy. I handed her the film. "Do you see what I see?" I asked.

Sandy looked at the picture of the window. "My God, who are those people?" she asked.

We both looked at the images of two older men. All we saw were their faces.

They were bearded and they wore hats. They looked like a couple of Orthodox Jews. I stood up excitedly. I looked at the comer of the window panel, where these images had appeared on film. I could see nothing, just the window. I took three more pictures.

Sandy and I watched as the images developed, one by one. Each picture had different faces. We both saw the faces; they were of both men and women. Most of the men had beards. I shot the entire roll. I had no more film or flashbulbs. Neither Sandy nor I was frightened by the experience. It was eerie but not scary.

As we looked at the first picture we had taken, we noticed that the faces were starting to fade. As the minutes went by, the other faces started to fade, too. We could still make them out but they were no longer clear.

It was three a.m. Sandy went to sleep. I told her I wasn't tired and that if anything else exciting were to happen, I would wake her up.

I stayed up until dawn, but nothing else happened. I went to bed and got a few hours sleep. When I woke up, Sandy was in the breakfast room. We looked at the pictures. They were just pictures of the window. There were no clear faces. I went out selling.

I came home early that afternoon, carrying a paper bag.

"What's that?" Sandy asked.

I showed her the contents of the bag.

I had bought ten rolls of Polaroid film and the flashbulbs to go with them.

"You know, I was doing some thinking on the way home. I remember this article I once read about this professor that's doing research on ESP. I'm going to find out who he is and write him a letter."

"Oh, you mean Dr. Rhine, the parapsychologist at Duke University."

I stood and looked at Sandy. I smiled and shook my head. "You little fuck, you know everything."

I picked up the receiver of the wall phone in the kitchen. "Who are you calling?" Sandy asked.

"The public library to get the city and state for Duke University."

"It's in Durham, North Carolina."

I shook my head. Where does that little fuck store all that information, I thought.

I got the long-distance operator, and finally the phone number for Duke University.

I asked the university switchboard operator for the address. "Is it possible to speak with Dr. Rhine?" I continued.

"Let me try his office."

"Dr. Rhine," the voice answered.

I introduced myself. I told him the story about the pictures and faces in the window. I did not tell him about the object that I thought was my soul, nor did I tell him about the picture of what was either Sandy or I from centuries ago. After all, I didn't want him to think he was talking to some nut. Sandy stood eagerly by my side as I spoke.

"These faces, these people...are they trying to communicate with you and your wife?"

"I'm sorry, would you say that again, Dr. Rhine?"

"I asked if they are trying to communicate with you."

"Just a moment, Dr. Rhine."

I put my hand over the receiver. I held back the laughter.

"Sandy," I whispered, "this guy is crazier than us...he wants to know if they're trying to communicate with us."

Sandy shook her head in disbelief.

"Would you like to speak to my wife, Dr. Rhine?"

"Yes."

Sandy introduced herself. She repeated the description of the faces. She explained how we had not noticed any attempts at communication ...that they were just pictures of faces. When she was through she returned the phone to me.

Dr. Rhine told me about a professor at a university in Japan, who a few years before, had reported experiences similar to what I had described. I was very interested in knowing more about this professor.

"What happened to him?" I asked.

"I don't know. He was released from the university and I never heard from him again."

"Oh," I said.

Dr. Rhine asked if I would send a few of the pictures I had taken. I explained that there was nothing left on them but the breakfast room window. A few of the pictures had the remnants of some faded faces. He asked that I mail him a report of what had happened, along with a few specimens of the faded pictures. Dr. Rhine also asked me to contact an associate at the University of Chicago and have him come over to our apartment so he could send a report after investigating the matter.

"Does the University of Chicago have a parapsychology department?" I asked.

"No, but the man I want you to meet is interested in the field, and I respect his judgment."

I wrote down the man's name and phone number and said good-bye to Dr. Rhine.

It was still not dark outside. I loaded the Polaroid and started shooting pictures of the window. A few of the pictures showed images of faces as they developed. But they weren't clear like those of the previous evening. Sandy started shooting pictures of the window. She got the same result, faded images but nothing clear.

I called the man whose name Dr. Rhine had given me. I introduced myself and went through the conversation I'd had with Dr. Rhine. He was very interested in coming to visit. We set a date for two days later. He was to arrive at nine and planned on staying late.

As the hours passed, Sandy fed our son and put him to bed in his crib. We sat in the kitchen and took pictures; they were clear for anyone to see, always different pictures. I took pictures of the windows of all the rooms in the house. Only the windows in the breakfast room and living room showed the faces. The breakfast table was covered with developed film. Over half of the pictures showed faces. We were excited about Dr. Rhine's associate coming to our apartment in two days.

Sandy was tired, and she went to bed. I sat in the breakfast room, the Polaroid on the table. I thought about spirits and ghosts and things of that nature. I asked myself what I'd do if a ghost appeared-would I run? Absolutely not! With a camera at hand, I'd want to take a picture. I was too curious about those faces in the window. I was too curious about that picture last week of Sandy or me from the distant past.

I was looking at the window, seeing nothing- just the building across the backyard and the tall apartment complex beyond. My gaze became fixed on a lighted apartment in the tall building. I squinted, narrowing my vision towards the light in the apartment building. The light went off. I laughed. Perfect timing, I thought. I tried it again on another lighted apartment. Nothing happened. This is ridiculous, I thought, I'm tired and I'm getting punchy. I'm going to go to bed.

Sandy was asleep. Our bedroom window on the first floor looked out over the back yard and toward the tall building. My side of the bed was closest to the window; lying on my left side, I would see the high-rise building and the lighted apartments. I squinted and narrowed my vision toward a lighted apartment on a high floor. I focused just on that light. By focusing steadily with my eyes squinted, I created a strain on the muscles around my eyes. After a short time, I could feel the muscles vibrating. I found I could look at just the center of what created the brightest part of that room, and then by squinting tighter without closing my eyes more, I would increase the tension against the muscles, which would then increase their vibrations. I was able to move my head ever so slightly, moving my eyes with my head, maintaining the direction of my gaze. A ray of light from a light bulb that was the center of brightness in that room followed the movement of my head. That ray of light now became the center of brightness for my eyes. By steadily focusing my vision into that ray of light, I was able to see into what appeared to be another dimension. I saw what appeared to be many naked, hairless men, visible from their waist up. Their arms were raised, and they swayed as in some type of ritual. I closed my eyes for a few seconds, and when I opened them again everything was normal. I thought about what had just happened, finally deciding that because of not getting enough sleep, I was probably making something out of nothing, and I went to sleep.

In the morning, just before going out selling, I told Sandy about my experience.

That evening we took more pictures, and we got more faces. It was kind of exciting strange but not frightening.

As Sandy slept later that evening, I lay on the bed and repeated the squinting and focusing of my eyes on a light bulb in a different apartment in the same tall building. As I looked into what I assumed to be another dimension, I saw people at a distance but could not distinguish who they were -or what they were doing. I was not hallucinating; this ability to see into another space within our universe was real. I had questioned the experience of the previous evening because I was tired and thought that perhaps my mind or eyes were playing tricks on me. This time I had had a good night's sleep and my mind was clear; what was happening now was a result of some new ability I had developed.

Tomorrow I would tell Sandy about this. I couldn't tell anyone else, not even Dr. Rhine's associate. It was just too crazy for anyone to believe.

The following morning before leaving for work, I told Sandy about my experience.

I explained how I had absolutely no way of proving what I had seen.

"Perhaps, after Dr. Rhine's associate leaves later tonight, I'll show you how I do it and maybe you can do it too."

"Sherwin, you want me to squint and look at a light bulb at a distance?"

"Well, it's more than squinting...you have to get the eye muscles to vibrate."

"You're crazy, Sherwin," Sandy laughed.

"I'll see you later tonight." I kissed her good-bye.

A few minutes past nine that evening our doorbell rang. It was Gerald Allen, Dr. Rhine's friend and associate. He was in his forties, wore a three-piece suit and horn rimmed glasses, and was a little pudgy. He was very polite and proper. We sat in the living room and Sandy asked if he would like coffee or something to drink.

"What do you have?" Gerald asked.

"We have Coke, ginger ale or orange juice," Sandy said. He looked disappointed.

"Would you like hard liquor?" I asked.

His eyes lit up and he started to look more comfortable. "Yes, what do you have?"

"We have vodka, gin, or scotch."

"Scotch will be just fine."

"How do you like it?" I asked.

"Over the rocks, just a little ice."

I went into the kitchen and retrieved an unopened fifth of Cutty Sark. I fixed his drink and brought a cup of black coffee for Sandy. We talked briefly about Dr. Rhine and how Gerald had known him for years and had helped investigate other matters of the paranormal for him. We talked about his affiliation with the University of Chicago. He changed the subject and asked what I did for a living. I explained that I had a small insurance agency. He became very interested in hearing about my business, picking my brain about what I thought regarding several different approaches to the marketing of insurance products. I was flattered that he complimented my answers to his questions.

But hell, I just had a real small insurance agency, and I couldn't understand his interest in my opinion. Gerald went to explain that he had gotten an assignment from a large national insurance company to write a marketing plan for them. I ascertained that he had probably landed it because of his academic credentials and that he probably didn't know what the fuck he was doing. I wanted to get off the subject and back to the purpose of his visit. I was confused by what his apparent credentials for writing a marketing plan and having an

111

assignment as a consultant for an insurance company had to do with Dr. Rhine and the field of parapsychology.

Gerald asked if he could have a refill. I took his empty glass to the kitchen and brought it back filled almost to the top with just a little ice.

"Can I take off my jacket?" he asked.

"Sure," Sandy replied.

He laid his jacket over the arm of the couch and loosened his tie. We started talking about psychology, philosophy and religion. The conversation was stimulating. Sandy was sitting across from the couch on which Gerald and I were sitting. We faced each other in a relaxed posture as we exchanged views on the world's great thinkers. Gerald Allen was extremely well read...he knew about everything. I was impressed. I had read an awful lot in recent months. But there was so much more that I not only had not read, but that I knew nothing at all about. I listened very carefully as he talked about different philosophies, religions and psychology. We exchanged ideas and opinions. Most of my input was an extension of what Gerald explained. And I was able to bring it to a deeper level. He was impressed. Sandy was enjoying watching the two of us. Gerald asked for another drink.

"Sandy, would you just bring the rest of the bottle of scotch here?" I asked.

"Yeah, that's a great idea, Sherwin," Gerald said.

Sandy returned with the almost empty fifth of scotch plus another unopened bottle and a small ice bucket full of ice. We had those two fifths left over from our bar at the coach house when we got married.

Gerald went to the bathroom. I looked at Sandy.

"Sandy, you know, if I had his intellectual knowledge of all the books he has read, I'd be dangerous."

Sandy laughed. "He sure drinks a lot," she said.

112

"Yeah, and he's not even drunk. He looks and sounds as sober as when he walked in." I laughed.

Gerald returned. He poured himself another drink. "Sherwin, there's a book you should read."

"What's that?"

"Science and Sanity by Alfred Korzybski."

"What's that about?" I was waiting for Sandy to come up with the answer...she didn't.

"Semantics," Gerald said.

"What's semantics?" I asked.

"The study of language. Get the book, Sherwin. I think you'll enjoy it. I had trouble understanding it, but it's worth reading."

"Do you guys know what time it is?" Sandy asked.

I looked at my watch.

"Wow, it's one o'clock already," I said.

"Let me see those pictures you took," Gerald said.

The three of us walked into the breakfast room. We sat at the table and I showed Gerald a few of the pictures that still had slight traces of images. They showed nothing conclusive and I stood up and shot a picture of the window. The three of us anxiously watched as the Polaroid film developed before our eyes. Nothing...just a picture of the window. I shot two rolls of film. Sandy and I were disappointed and a little embarrassed. No faces showed on the film.

"Gerald, I don't know what to tell you. This is just an off night. We've had it before", I said.

We returned to the living room, and as we sat down there was a knock at the door. "I wonder who that is?" Sandy asked.

"I don't know. I'll get it."

I opened the front door. It was our upstairs neighbor Bobbie, the go-go dancer. "What are you guys doing up so late? I saw your lights on...can I come in?"

"Sure, come on in, Bobbie," I said.

Bobbie and Sandy were glad to see each other. We introduced Bobbie to Gerald; I thought his eyes were going to pop out of their sockets when Bobbie took off her coat and sat down in her work costume. Bobbie was as bubbly and full of life as ever. She had just returned from her job at the Velvet Swing on the Near North Side. Besides dancing and serving drinks, part of her job was to sit on a red velvet seat above the crowd and swing back and forth over the bar.

I gave Bobbie a scotch and soda; Gerald poured himself another scotch with no ice, Sandy had coffee and I had a Coke.

Bobbie finally said good night and went upstairs to her apartment. Gerald left about fifteen minutes later. I told him I would call again to get together.

It had been an interesting evening of conversation; it was fun, but nothing happened that would be of interest to Dr. Rhine. Sandy and I went to sleep.

The following week, I picked up the book Gerald had recommended. It kept me up for many hours for several weeks. Every evening I would read and lecture to Sandy.

My thoughts about the true meaning of many of the books I had previously read having been lost in their translation were validated.

We would still take pictures of the window every evening, and we always saw the faces appear as the film developed.

One late evening while sitting alone in the breakfast room, I saw strange flashes of light coming from the second floor of the three-story apartment building across our back yard. Sandy and Bobbie were in the living room talking. It was Bobbie's night off; her mother and aunt were out of town and she was alone. I turned off the light in the breakfast room and stood looking at the rear room of the apartment across our yard. I felt there was someone watching me and that perhaps he had a flashlight in his dimly lit room. I couldn't tell. I called Sandy and Bobbie into the darkened breakfast room and asked if they could see anybody or flashes of light from the second floor across the yard. The three of us stood in silence. No one saw anything, except perhaps light reflections from a nearby street lamp. I asked Bobbie if we could go to her apartment, directly above ours, so I could see better. Like three high-school kids we ran up to Bobbie's apartment and stood in her darkened breakfast room looking at the room across the yard. We had our noses pressed against the window, hoping to find some peeping tom.

Bobbie seemed a little scared. We saw nothing, just the dimly lit room with no one there. We stood at Bobbie's front door saying good night.

"Wait a few minutes," I said. "I'm going back there to take one last look."

I entered Bobbie's darkened breakfast room. I stood and looked across the yard into the second-floor room. What I saw sent a shiver up and down my spine. Sitting in that room in a high-backed wicker chair by the window was a man. He wore a black turban and a suit and tie. He had a dark beard and mustache, and in the center of his forehead was what appeared to be a shining black jewel. My first impression was that I was looking at a mystical Egyptian priest sitting on a throne....I didn't know; he was really spooky. In astonishment, I stared at this mystical man for several minutes as he looked out the window, and then I turned to summon Sandy and Bobbie.

"Quick, quick," I softly called, "there's someone there. Hurry, hurry," I urged.

I looked across the yard. The man stood up and walked away from the wicker chair. Sandy and Bobbie entered the room and rushed to the window. No one was there. No one was sitting in the wicker chair. I told them what had happened, what I had seen.

"Sherwin, you're scaring the hell out of me. I'm not going to be able to sleep," Bobbie said.

I giggled as I saw the absurdity in this whole thing. Sandy giggled. Bobbie giggled. She had regained her composure. I explained to Bobbie about the spirit faces Sandy and I had been taking pictures of. I told her about Duke University and Dr. Rhine and about Gerald being sent to our apartment to investigate.

"That man across the yard that I just saw...he must be responsible for all that has been happening," I said.

"Sherwin, you're scaring the hell out of me again," Bobbie said.

"Bobbie, come downstairs with us. We'll take pictures and show you the faces," I said.

"Sandy, is Sherwin pulling my leg?" Bobbie asked.

"No, come downstairs and we'll show you," Sandy said.

"You're both crazy," Bobbie laughed.

I giggled. Sandy giggled.

"Bobbie, go to sleep. Sandy and I have to go back down. Matthew is all alone," I said.

"I'll be sleeping under the covers tonight," Bobbie said.

"Good night," Sandy and I echoed.

The next morning, I drove Sandy to the office. We talked about the mysterious man I had seen. I explained again that I had first thought he was Egyptian, but then thought that he might be from Baghdad and that I really didn't know. I couldn't get over the shining jewel in his forehead...the whole scene was just bizarre. I dropped Sandy off and I went out selling.

Several days passed. Then one night, returning from the office, we were walking from the car to the apartment. On the corner of our side of the street was a large fenced in empty lot. In the lot near the fence was a lighted billboard. As we passed near the billboard, I stopped suddenly. I grabbed Sandy's arm to get her to stop. We both looked in amazement at the bottom right corner on the billboard. There before us were two of the faces we had taken a picture of the previous evening. We

116

couldn't believe what we were seeing. I was hoping someone would walk by, so I could stop them and ask, "Excuse me, sir or madam ...but do you see those faces on the corner of the billboard?"

But the street was deserted. Just Sandy and I alone, looking at those faces. "Sherwin, what's that French word for craziness for two?"

"Folie a deux," I answered.

"I think that's what we have," she said seriously.

We went into our apartment; the housekeeper left. I didn't want to get her involved in this spirit picture stuff. We would have spooked her out and she would have quit. We liked her; she was nice and reliable, and she loved taking care of our son.

Around nine that evening, we were both in the living room. I walked to the window to look outside. Across the street in front of our apartment was a grassy area bordered by trees. Something drew me to look in that direction.

"My God, my God," I uttered.

"What? What?" Sandy asked nervously.

"Those eyes, those eyes."

'What eyes?"

I heard Sandy approach to look out the window. I turned and grabbed her.

"Don't get near the window," I hollered. "Stay away from the window ...don't, don't look at those eyes." I walked us away from the window.

I was afraid to go back to the window. What I had seen had scared the living shit out of me.

"What did you see? What did you see?" Sandy exclaimed.

"Two large eyes. Two very large black eyes; they were almost glowing. They were trying to hypnotize me."

"Was there a body with the eyes?" Sandy asked.

"There must have been ...but all I could see were the big dark eyes. Just the eyes looking and staring at me. I think it's someone from outer space. There must be more of them across the street in the lot, hiding behind the trees."

I walked to the window. I stood sideways. I wouldn't look out; I just hurriedly pulled down the shades. I was really frightened. I sat on the couch next to Sandy. I was trying to think what I could do. I regained my composure, picked up the phone on the end table, stood up and dialed Information.

"The phone number of the FBI. It's an emergency," I said.

"What are you doing?" Sandy exclaimed.

"I'm calling the FBI. This is not a police matter," I said sternly.

"Sherwin, are you OK?"

"I'm fine...Just don't go near that window," I insisted.

"Thank you, operator," I said. I dialed the number.

A man answered. He gave his name and introduced himself as an agent. I introduced myself. I spoke very calmly. I didn't want the FBI to think they had a nut on the line.

"I know you're going to find this very difficult to believe...and let me assure you that this is not a hoax, but there are these two big dark black eyes in this empty lot across the street from my apartment. And these eyes are staring at me, trying to hypnotize me. I think it's someone from outer space... think there's more of them behind the trees. I have every reason to believe we are being invaded from outer space...Can you send some FBI agents over right away?" I gave him my name again, my address and phone number. I was proud of myself and my ability to speak so clearly and calmly under these hysterical conditions. As I awaited his answer, I saw Sandy's mouth was open; there were wrinkles in her forehead caused by the wideness of her eyes as she stared at me in disbelief.

"All right...if you're sure. Thank you very much," I said. I put down the receiver.

"What did he say?" Sandy asked incredulously. "

You're not going to believe this."

"What did he say?" Sandy repeated.

"He said it doesn't come under their jurisdiction and that I should call the department of the army."

I chuckled nervously. Sandy chuckled. It was obvious that he hadn't believed me. "Sherwin, you have to get some rest...you haven't been sleeping much. Please go to bed," Sandy urged.

"You're right," I said, "but promise me you won't go near the window."

"I promise."

I lay down in bed on my back. I had my shirt and pants on...I was frightened out of my wits. I turned the lamp off and turned on my side. I looked past the courtyard to the high-rise complex. I focused on a light bulb on one of the higher floors. I squinted, causing a vibration from the contraction of the muscles around my eyes. I was looking into another dimension. *My God, what is that?* I thought. I saw a large space inside of what looked like a cave or the inside of a mountain ...it was a large room. There was a platform of concrete with steps leading up to it. Lying on the platform was a body-a body of a very large man. The man was lying on his back. He was covered with a white linen or sheet from his feet up to the bottom of his hairless chest. The man's skin was of a ghostly whitish gray. His face was familiar, very familiar.

As I continued to gaze into the distant light bulb, I found I didn't have to squint as hard. I was able to squint ever so slightly and still see the room, the platform, the man. The vibration from the muscles stopped. I was looking at myself ...what I saw was me, my other me, my astral body. I was calm, entranced by what I was observing. The room was illuminated by natural light. At the far left corner and beyond the platform and head of what still seemed to be me was the opening of a tunnel like the entrance to this chamber where my other me lay. I noticed a figure walking out of the tunnel. It was a man. My

God, I thought, it's the man I saw several days before from Bobbie's apartment. He wore a black turban; he had a beard, a mustache. He wore a black suit, a black tie. The suit was of a style from the thirties or forties, or perhaps, I thought, just European and not in style in this country. Was I looking into another dimension or was I seeing some secret hidden place somewhere on earth? I didn't know. The man was not Egyptian, not an Iraqi from Baghdad. No, he looked like someone from India, a Sikh.

He walked into the huge chamber, the cave, the room ...whatever it was. The walls of the space were of stone. He walked closer within my view of the room. I saw him clearly, just as I could see my other me lying on the platform. He walked around to the stone steps leading up to the platform. He walked up the steps. He stood next to my head. His body was miniaturized next to the side of my other me. My other me had his eyes closed, as if asleep. The man from the other night had had a jewel in his forehead; this one didn't. Still, I wondered whether this was the same man; later, I realized it was. He was just a normal-looking Sikh; he could have been a businessman. He spoke into the ear of my other me. I couldn't hear what he said; I just saw his lips moving. He was giving my other me what appeared to be a healing of sorts with magical words.

That's all I remember. I woke up the next morning feeling fine. I had a sense of well being. I was relaxed. The fright and fear from the night before were gone. I was totally rested and happily at peace.

As I drove Sandy to the office, I told her the story. My words and descriptions of what I saw were magical to Sandy's ears. She believed.

I asked her what today's date was.

"April second," she said.

"What was yesterday?"

"April first."

"What else?" I softly asked.

"April Fool's Day," she said.

"Yes, and that guy from the FBI I talked to probably thought someone was trying to play an April Fool's Day joke." We both laughed.

Chapter 10

I could not get the man with the turban out of my mind. Whenever I talked about him to Sandy, I would refer to him as the man with the turban. Finally, I decided to give him a name. The Hebrew word for a pious and righteous man is *zaddik*. I liked the sound of the name but it did not describe the mystical man I had seen. This man was like a priest with magical powers who could travel between heaven and earth. I decided to call him the *Zadik* and spell it with only one *d*.

I couldn't tell anyone about the *Zadik*. I couldn't tell anyone about those two big black eyes across the street. I couldn't tell anyone about what happened when I squinted...no, all I could possibly tell anyone would be about the pictures that showed the faces, and about these I would tell only a select few.

I decided to call my cousin Deanie's husband. Marty used to be a professional photographer and he still had excellent camera equipment. If I could get him interested in spirit faces, I might be able to obtain some solid evidence for Dr. Rhine. I arranged to meet him for lunch. I brought along several of the pictures Sandy and I had taken, and although the faces were not as clear as originally shot, both Sandy and I could still distinguish some of them.

I had always enjoyed Marty's company, and I felt confident that he would see the images in the pictures. After all, he was a trained photographer. After our meal, I pulled out the pictures. I had told Marty that I wanted to show him some pictures but I had not discussed their contents.

I handed him one of the pictures.

"Marty, do you see anything unusual about this picture?" He held the Polaroid picture and studied it.

"Sherwin, it's a picture of a window. It looks like your breakfast room at your apartment."

"Yeah, I know...but right over here in the comer." I pointed.

"What do you see?" Marty looked again. He held the picture at a different angle.

"It's a picture of a window. What am I supposed to see?"

"Do you see the slight images of two faces?"

"Two faces...where?"

"OK, Marty...I have a few more pictures." I handed him four others. "Do you see any faces on any of these pictures?"

At this point, I could tell he was trying to be kind. What he probably wanted to say was, "Are you crazy or something?" I was beginning to feel uncomfortable and foolish. I was sorry I had shown him the pictures. I thought perhaps the faces were like the famous metamorphic picture where the eyes first see a skull and then adjust to see a lady at a dressing table holding a mirror in front of her face--or vice versa. But then I thought, no...those pictures were very clear when first shot. I was really disappointed at his not seeing the faces. I dropped the subject, and soon after, we left the restaurant and went our separate ways.

I got a Rolleiflex camera and started using that to take pictures. I was back on Methedrine on a daily schedule. I was getting very little sleep. I was reading about the Kabbalah into the wee hours of the morning. Sandy became disenchanted with the picture-taking and my taking Methedrine. She wanted to return to a normal way of life-away from the spirit faces and strange happenings. We started to argue. I became obsessed with trying to discover the unknown.

I received a letter from Dr. Rhine; apparently he didn't know his associate had already been to our apartment.

April 13, 1964

Mr. Sherwin Ernst 711 Montrose
Chicago, Illinois

Dear Mr. Ernst:
I have been watching my mail pile since I had the telephone call from you and Mrs. Ernst, expecting to have a report in writing about the interesting matters you mentioned to me by telephone. Has something happened to change your mind regarding putting this letter to me?

I should like, of course, to have an opportunity of looking over some of the specimens you mentioned, but perhaps you do not wish to trust these to the mails.

I do not know whether or not you got in touch with Mr. Gerald Allen. I have another friend who is going to Chicago soon, who would be interested in this matter if I were to tell him about it, but I do not wish to mention it unless there is no other way.

At any rate, if you are still interested in having us go into the matter with you, let me know. If not, I should appreciate a word as to just what your decision was.

Sincerely yours,
J.B. Rhine

I kept a log on what had happened. I planned to send Dr. Rhine a letter with some spirit images in the near future, if they developed well with my new camera.

One late afternoon, I was in the kitchen. I had just put out a cigarette. A piece of tobacco was on my left thumbnail. Becoming fascinated with this fleck of tobacco, I pulled out a large magnifying glass from the drawer of our breakfront in the dining room. I returned to the kitchen, where I stood and held the magnifying glass about six and a half inches above my thumb. I gazed through the lens and looked at that one fleck of tobacco resting on my thumbnail. Suddenly, everything within sight through that magnifying glass turned into a misty cloud. That one piece of tobacco stood on one end...It turned into a dinosaur. I was seeing a dinosaur surrounded by a misty cloud. I felt a voice speaking to me. It was the voice of either God or Moses. I felt, rather than heard, it explaining to me how the universe had existed eons ago. I felt the way Moses must have felt when he was given the commandments. I was in a state of intoxication. I was the one chosen by God to deliver His words to the world.

"Sandy, Sandy," I called out, "come quick, come quick." She hurried into the kitchen.

"God is speaking to me. God is speaking to me."

"You're hearing His voice?" she asked nervously.

"No, no...I'm feeling His voice. I'm feeling his voice throughout my body...Look, look through the magnifying glass...Look, look at the dinosaur on my thumb. Do you see it? Do you see it?"

Sandy looked.

"I do not see a dinosaur, Sherwin."

"Look, look again. ...see, see, it's there. "

She did not answer. She was quiet. I turned to look at her. Her eyes were red and filled with tears.

"Don't cry, Sandy. I've been chosen by God to deliver His words to the world. Don't cry...be happy!"

I turned to move closer to her and show her the dinosaur. It fell from my thumb.

"Hold this magnifying glass," I said.

I got on my knees to look for this fleck of tobacco to put back on my thumb, to again look through the lens to see the dinosaur. I couldn't find the tobacco.

"Help me. Help me find the tobacco," I pleaded.

I spent a considerable length of time on the kitchen floor looking for that one little piece of tobacco. I could not find it. I walked into the living room and sat on a chair. Sandy followed. I put my head in my palms. I cried.

"I'm going mad," I said. "Find a psychiatrist for me. I'm going crazy."

"Who should I call?" Sandy asked.

"Call Deanie. She'll find someone."

I was regaining my composure. Sandy was on the phone with my cousin Deanie. "Deanie wants to come over," Sandy said.

"No, I'll be OK...Just ask her to find a psychiatrist. I'll see him. I'm OK right now."

"Deanie will call back." Sandy put her arm around my shoulder. "Are you OK?"

"Yeah, I'm OK now. Can you believe that? I'm on my fucking hands and knees looking for a fucking dinosaur on the floor. I can't believe I did that" I grinned in disbelief. "Get me a soft drink, would you please? I'm dying of thirst."

Sandy went to the kitchen. The phone rang. Sandy picked it up. She returned with the soft drink about ten minutes later.

"That was Deanie. She gave me the name and phone number of a psychiatrist in Skokie. He's supposed to be very good."

"Where did she find out about him?" I asked.

"Through a friend whose father he's treating. He supposedly helped a lot." "What's his name?"

"Sam Stein."

"Call him and set up an appointment. I'll see him."

Early the following morning, I was in Dr. Stein's office. I filled out the information sheet and waited. It was only five minutes before I was shown into his private office.

Dr. Stein was a stout man in his fifties with graying hair. After the introduction and his reading my fact sheet, he noted,

126

"Your wife said you have been taking Methedrine." He was familiar with the drug.

"Yes."

"How much have you been taking?"

"Four cc's a day."

"You're taking it injectably?"

"Yes."

"How did you get the drug?"

"I'd rather not say."

He respected my answer and started to make notes. I gave him a brief bio of my adoption, the picture-taking and the experience I'd had the previous night. I referred to God or Moses talking to me as either a vision or a hallucination.

"Your wife said you saw a dinosaur on your thumb. Do you think that was a vision?"

"My intellect tells me that was a hallucination." "Have you had other hallucinations?"

"No."

"Have you had other visions?"

"No."

"Your wife told me you said that you can see another dimension." "I can look into another dimension under the right circumstances."

"How do you do that?"

I explained the eye squinting and all the experiences I'd had. I explained the picture spirits, the Dr. Rhine story. I did not omit anything.

"Sherwin, the first thing you're going to have to do is stop taking Methedrine."

"I stopped as of last night," I laughed. "The dinosaur on my thumbnail was the coup de gras."

I finally got him to smile.

We set another appointment for the following morning. I was told to see his nurse to have blood drawn before leaving.

Dr. Stein's office in Skokie was a small one-story building that he occupied alone. He had a receptionist; the nurse was his wife. The building also had a laboratory, which Stein used for his research in the field of biochemistry. He occasionally lectured at Roosevelt University, just south of downtown Chicago, and had many published articles in the field of psychiatry. He gave me prescriptions for twelve different drugs. Most of the pills were extremely tiny and were given to correct a chemical imbalance from which I suffered, according to Stein. He always gave me reprints of his published articles, rubber-stamped "With the compliments of the author, Sam I. Stein, Ph. D., M. D. "

I considered him to be an egotist; however, I did enjoy our visits. It was not your typical doctor-patient encounter; instead, it was as if I was a student taking a course in physiology. He would talk and show me pictures of the human brain and how the nervous systems can create chemical imbalances under certain conditions. I would always bring faded spirit pictures from the previous nights to our sessions, and I showed Stein the letter from Dr. Rhine asking that I write or send specimens. I told Stein that I was going to write to Rhine and let him know that I still hadn't gotten any photos that I felt might be of interest. Stein asked if he could write to Rhine on my behalf. I hesitated, but agreed it would be all right for him to send a letter. Stein did not show an interest in either my pictures or my previous experiences. I considered stopping my visits; however, I didn't because of the lectures on physiology and chemical imbalances, within the brain. I was fascinated by the new knowledge I was absorbing. However, I did start taking Methedrine again without Stein's or Sandy's knowledge.

The friction between Sandy and me had intensified. She saw Stein. He suggested she take L-tryptophan for depression. She felt despair in having noticed no change, after five weeks, in my obsession with the picture taking, which she felt distanced us from what she considered a normal way of life. Hell, I was a kook when she met me. I hadn't changed; she was the one who had changed. We used to enjoy taking the pictures together and watching the faces slowly appear as the film developed. Now, I was alone in my quest for answers. We grew apart. One night, we had a violent argument about Stein. I told her I was going to stop seeing him. Her reaction was one of incredulity. I walked into the bathroom and emptied all twelve bottles of Stein's pills into the toilet.

The bathroom door was open. I wanted Sandy to see. "What are you doing?" she screamed from the bedroom.

My thumb rested on the chrome-plated handle. "What does it look like I'm doing? I'm flushing that egomaniac Stein's fucking pills down the fucking toilet."

She ran into the bathroom to stop me. It was already too late. The last of the pills had sunk to the bottom of the toilet bowl. I pushed my thumb down on the handle and flushed them away. "Chicago River, here I come," I said sarcastically.

That was the last straw. Sandy went apeshit. She struck out, she pounded my arms, my chest; she bit my body and kicked me in the shins. Her nails were going for my face when I grabbed her hands, pulled her into the bedroom and flung her onto the bed.

"Keep your fucking hands off me, bitch," I hollered.

I grabbed a suitcase out of the closet and began to pack. "What are you doing?" she shouted.

"I'm getting the fuck out of here."

"Where are you going?"

"I don't know...I'm just going," I answered angrily. I packed just the bare necessities and marched to the front door. Sandy ran out of the bedroom and blocked the door with her body and outstretched arms.

"Don't you leave!" she screamed in my face.

I grabbed her upper arms, forcing them down, and lifted her body out of my way. She was back in a flash, blocking my exit.

"Bastard. Don't leave, bastard. You're not leaving!" she exclaimed angrily. I thought: I tower over her and this little fuck is keeping me from leaving?

"Shit. " I put the suitcase back down and walked away. She didn't follow...she had won the first round.

Later she came into the dining room where I lay on the daybed with my head buried in my arms, escaping her insanity.

"Look what you did to my arms," she exclaimed, as she showed me the bruises I had inflicted with my grip.

I slightly raised my head and squinted at her bruised arms. "Go away. Will you please," I softly whispered.

She left the room in a huff and slammed the bedroom door closed. I fell asleep on the daybed and left early the next morning, before she had awakened, to go out selling.

When I returned home that Monday evening, it was just turning dark. I opened the front door, and sitting in my living room were my cousins Deanie and Shirley. I was very surprised to see them there.

"What are you guys doing here?" I asked.

"Oh, we were just in the neighborhood and thought we'd stop by," Deanie said. Shirley echoed a similar greeting.

"Where's Sydney and Marty?" I asked. They said their husbands would be there soon.

"Where's Sandy?"

"Sandy took Matthew out; they'll be back soon," Shirley replied.

I shrugged my shoulders, excused myself and went into the kitchen to be alone for a while. I was exhausted from last night and was sorry they were there, as I was in no mood for conversation.

A short time later, the doorbell rang. I assumed it was Marty or Sydney. I walked through the hallway, opened the front door and prepared to buzz open the lobby door. It was neither Marty nor Sydney. It was two uniformed men, an ambulance driver and an attendant, carrying a stretcher.

I walked down the few steps and opened the lobby door. I could see the ambulance in front of the building.

"Yes, can I help you?" I asked.

"Yes, we have a pick-up order for Sherwin-" He was having trouble pronouncing my last name.

"Let me see that paper you're holding," I demanded incredulously. "What the hell is this?" I hollered.

"Is this you?" they both asked.

"Yes," I said. "Get the fuck out of here."

I ran back upstairs. One of them held the lobby door open with the stretcher, and the other followed me up to my front door.

"We have a pick-up order for you from a Dr. Sam Stein to take you to Forest Hospital in Des Plaines."

I stood at my front door. I would not let them in the apartment.

"Get the fuck out of here or I'll bash your fucking heads in!" I hollered.

I slammed the door in their faces. I turned to Deanie, Shirley and Marty, who by this time had come in. "What the hell's going on here...where's Sandy?" I demanded.

Everyone was now standing in the living room in silence.

"She's not here," Shirley said.

"I know that," I angrily stated. "Where is she?"

My cousins and Marty tried to talk me into going in the ambulance, saying that Dr. Stein wanted me in the hospital.

"What the fuck did Sandy tell Stein?" I hollered.

There was a forceful knock at the door. I opened it, prepared to throw these two assholes' tails out into the street.

It was two uniformed police officers from the Chicago Police Department "What's going on here?" they asked.

"These two guys have a pick-up order to take me to a hospital from a Dr. Stein, who was lied to by my crazy wife," I exclaimed.

The police officers asked the ambulance people to show them the paper. They studied the pick-up order.

"This pick-up order is not legal here in Chicago. This is only good in Des Plaines." Discouraged, the driver and attendant left.

"Thank you, officers," I said.

They left. I went into the living room. Sydney was there; he must have entered during the excitement and I hadn't noticed.

"What's going on?" Sydney asked.

"Ask them!" I looked at Deanie, Shirley and Marty in total disgust. I slammed the door and left. I got into my white Chevrolet and drove to the drugstore to call Stein. I wanted to see him now! I was furious. I thought: That total asshole, Stein, must have listened to that crazy soon to be ex-wife of mine with some bullshit story about our fight last night. I couldn't believe Stein would buy that bullshit. I couldn't believe Deanie, Shirley, Marty and Sydney would buy that bullshit. How could Deanie and Shirley, my Wicker Park cousins, allow this to happen? It was unbelievable.

I called Stein's office from the drugstore pay phone. His answering service took the call.

"What's Dr. Stein's home phone number?" I calmly asked. "I'm one of his patients and I have to talk to him right away."

"I'm sorry, we're not allowed to give out his home phone number. May I take a message?"

"That's OK, thanks." I hung up and dialed Information. He had an unlisted phone number in Skokie. I asked for the number under his wife's name. It was listed. I dialed. A man's voice answered, "Hello." I recognized Stein's voice.

"Dr. Stein, this is Sherwin. What the fuck is going on?" I hollered.

"Sherwin, your wife said you're violent and that you threw away your pills."

"I'm violent?" I screamed. "That fucking bitch would have scratched my eyes out last night if I didn't stop her...what's your fucking home address? I'm coming over to see you. We have to talk this over now."

"Where are you now?" he asked.

"I'm at a drugstore in Chicago."

He hesitated. "Meet me at my office in forty minutes."

"Fine." I slammed the phone down.

I got in my car and headed for his office in Skokie. This time of night, traffic was light; it would be about a thirty-minute ride. I calmed down. I was thinking about what I was going to tell Stein. I couldn't believe he had bought into her bullshit about my being violent. She's the crazy one...not me. I wondered if she had done it because of that affair with Audrey. I was going to tell Stein about that. As far as throwing away the pills, I wasn't gonna be seeing him any more anyway. I didn't need a doctor.

I looked at my watch. I wasn't far from his office and I would be ten minutes early. I stopped at the Cock Robin restaurant to pick up two cups of coffee for Stein and me to drink while we talked. There was a small crowd standing in line to place their orders. I was soon out of the restaurant carrying a brown bag with two Styrofoam cups of coffee. I had just placed my key in the ignition switch when I was suddenly surrounded by four police cars with flashing lights. Uniformed officers converged on me and my car. I was ordered out with my hands raised. Their hands rested on their holsters. They seemed disappointed that I didn't have a weapon.

"Are you Sherwin-?" They mispronounced my last name. I corrected their pronunciation.

"Yes," I said.

"Put your hands on top of your car," they ordered.

133

They frisked me as you would frisk any typical most-wanted. They searched the car. They opened the brown bag, expecting to find TNT. They seemed disappointed with the only evidence being two cups of non-explosive coffee. They ordered me into the back seat of one of the patrol cars. I watched the crowd staring at me as I was whisked away in a procession of flashing lights. I was speechless. In disbelief I sat alone in the locked caged rear seat of a Skokie police patrol car. The procession pulled into Stein's office building parking lot. The building's lights were on and I was escorted into Stein's office surrounded by what appeared to be the entire Skokie police department. The words fuck, shit, bastard, cocksucker, son-of-a-bitch were no longer part of my vocabulary.

"Dr. Stein," I calmly asked, "what is going on?"

"You're violent, Sherwin, and you're going to the hospital. There is an ambulance on the way."

I looked for the police officer with the most stripes.

"Am I allowed to call my attorney?" I asked.

He hesitated for a moment and then said, "Sure."

My cousin, Melvin, the one who has an office in my building, the one who told Sandy I was adopted, lived in Skokie. The sergeant handed me the phone book I had requested, and I looked for Melvin's name. I dialed his number.

"Melvin," I said, "this is your cousin, Sherwin...I'm fine...No, as a matter of fact, I'm not fine." I calmly explained the current situation. I kept the facts down to five minutes. Melvin asked to speak to the sergeant in charge.

When the sergeant was through speaking with my cousin, I was given back the phone. "Sherwin, I'll try and get you out tomorrow ...I can't do anything tonight."

I was still calm. I always knew I would have made an incredible actor, and this would have been the best role I could have ever played.

"OK, Melvin, see what you can do." I hung up.

"Dr. Stein," I asked, "am I going to see you in the hospital tomorrow?"

"No," Stein replied, "I will not be seeing you again. Another doctor will see you tomorrow in the hospital."

The ambulance arrived and two men wearing white shirts laid a stretcher on the hallway floor. They asked me to lie down on the stretcher. The Skokie police surrounded me, awaiting my final desperate attempt at freedom. I lay down on the stretcher. They strapped me in tightly and placed me in the ambulance, and off I went to Stein's Funny Farm-Forest Hospital in Des Plaines, another suburb about a twenty minute ride farther away. As I lay strapped to the stretcher in the ambulance that hurriedly drove off, flashing its lights and sounding its siren, I was in total disbelief. My anger was gone, my sense of humor was gone, my self-respect was gone.

The ambulance arrived at the hospital and I was carried on the stretcher into a small room. The attendants unstrapped me and left me alone.

They closed and locked the solid door and I sat on the edge of the cot in the dimly lit, bare-walled room, wondering what was next. I couldn't believe Deanie and Shirley had allowed Sandy and Stein to do this. I felt no anger. Just disbelief. My only hope was that my cousin Melvin would have me out in the morning. A male attendant and a female nurse entered. I was given two sleeping pills; the only words spoken were by the nurse: "A doctor will see you in the morning." The door slammed closed again.

I thought about what I would say to the doctor in the morning. I knew Sandy hadn't done this for revenge because of my affair with Audrey, but I would lie and say she had. I would tell about my affair. After all, I thought, Sandy had lied to Stein, for he accused me of being violent and it was always she who started and provoked the fights and arguments. I just

135

wanted to take my pictures; if I got on her nerves, that was her problem, not mine. I just wanted to be left alone in my quest for the unknown ...She always had her face in my face with words of anger about my obsession in search of the truth. It was she who always struck out; I only defended myself. I never did hit her or hurt her. The bruises on her arms were from my holding her arms down so I could get out the door. Sandy was wild. Sandy was the crazy one, not me. I would tell about my taking Methedrine, and that would explain my obsession ...it would explain the dinosaur and other happenings. Yes, I thought, I'll blame the unknown on Methedrine. I'll say that I had already stopped taking the drug...I'll just be calm and rational. I was calm and rational as I thought this through ...Between my convincing the new doctor, and Melvin's legal help, I'd be out by early afternoon, and then I'd go home, pack and move out. I'd have Deanie and Shirley there. That way Sandy couldn't try and stop me, and if she did, Deanie and Shirley would see the truth. I had it all decided: I do not want to be married to Sandy...she is a mental case and I don't have time for her bullshit I'm going to split from her! With those thoughts, I fell asleep.

At eight o'clock the next morning, after I'd been taken out for lab tests and x-rays and returned to my room, there was a knock and the door opened. A smartly dressed woman wearing a blue jacket smiled and introduced herself as the doctor assigned to my case. She examined me and we sat on my bed and talked. She wrote notes on a clipboard. I felt at ease with her. I always felt at ease with nice-looking women. I explained about the misunderstanding with Stein about who had created the violence. I explained about my taking Methedrine and all the other thoughts I'd had before falling asleep last night. She seemed very nice and told me I would be able to walk around the inside of the building during the day. And the door would not be kept locked in my pleasant new room that I'd move into tomorrow.

"In a few days, you may walk around the grounds," she said.

"Are you saying I can't leave today?" I asked.

"No. You'll have to stay until we can do a complete evaluation." She tried to get me to sign admission papers. I refused.

She called for the nurse and instructed her to show me around the area. "I'll see you tomorrow morning," the doctor said.

The nurse showed me the section of the hospital my room was in. It was attractively furnished with a recreational room; outside was a beautiful manicured lawn. It was like an estate or resort. I was given breakfast and allowed to roam at will-except I couldn't go out onto the lawn area yet. The other patients wandered freely throughout the building, smiling at me as they passed. They were well dressed and seemed intelligent; apparently they or their families could afford what seemed to be an expensive place. Everyone was cheerful...except me. I went to the nurses' station and asked if I could make a phone call.

"Sorry, but it will be a few days before you can use a telephone," the nurse replied pleasantly.

I looked at the nurse's name tag on her blouse and repeated her name. "What I want to do is write a letter to the Exchange National Bank in Chicago, taking my bookkeeper's name off the authorization for signing checks for my business."

The nurse looked up.

"I suggest you find someone in charge of the hospital and repeat what I just said...otherwise this hospital is going to have a lawsuit on their hands." My voice was controlled but firm.

"Excuse me, I'll be right back." She hurriedly left, disappearing around the far comer. A few minutes later, she returned and asked me to follow her. I walked by her side down a long corridor to a business office. It was nice to hear the sound of typewriters and see a business office. A man came out of a private office and asked what I wanted. I asked his name, which I repeated.

"I would like a pencil, paper, and an envelope to write the vice president who handles my business checking account at the Exchange National Bank."

"Why?" he asked.

"To take the name of my bookkeeper off the signing of any checks while I am illegally incarcerated in this hospital." I paused and repeated the man's name. "I suggest this letter goes out today; otherwise this hospital will be sued when I get out." The tone of my voice was very firm.

He reacted quickly, handing me a plain sheet of typing paper and a plain white envelope. He watched as I printed, in correct business form, the name of the vice president of the Exchange National Bank, and the name of my company.

Re: ---

Dear Ted:

Effective immediately, please rescind Marshall's signature authorization to sign any of my business checking accounts. I will call you for lunch upon my return to Chicago.

Yours truly,

I signed my name as president. I showed him the letter before folding and placing it in the addressed envelope. I repeated his name and said, "I suggest you make sure this goes out in today's mail."

"It will go out today," he assured me.

The nurse escorted me back to my assigned area. If Melvin doesn't get me out, that letter will shake Sandy up, I thought. They're not going to be able to run that fucking business without me.

I felt good about the first punch I had delivered. That fucking Stein is going to get hit with such a lawsuit when I get out, he won't know what hit him, I thought. And Sandy...I'm leaving her.

I was approached by a nurse. "You have a visitor," she said.

I smiled. At last...Melvin, my cousin, my attorney, my savior, had arrived.

I enthusiastically followed the nurse to the visitor's lounge. I was unshaven, my pants and shirt wrinkled, my hair uncombed, but I felt good as I entered the lounge.

Then I felt the look of disappointment on my face. It was my cousin Shirley. She walked toward me, all smiles.

"Sherwin, you look wonderful," she said as she kissed my cheek. "Sandy wanted to come but she was afraid you wouldn't want to see her. But I told her that next week you would want her to come visit and I would drive her."

I repeated to myself, "Next week...Sandy, next week...Sandy, Sandy, Sandy," as I stood looking at Shirley, my face reddening. I could feel the blood rush into my face. The words that were not part of my vocabulary the previous night at Stein's office burst forth tenfold as I shouted in a mad rage.

"That Fuck, that Shit, that Bitch, that Asshole, that Cocksucker, that Bastard, that Son-of-a-bitch, that Motherfucker ...I'll kill her, I'll kill her, I'll kill her!" I shouted out every conceivable secret I knew about Sandy. I made up things about her that were not true...I wanted Sandy destroyed. Shirley felt the force and heat of my anger. She was aghast, frightened as she'd never been. The noblest of saints would have been scared.

An attendant and a nurse rushed toward me. Everyone in the visitor's lounge was silent, staring with open mouths, wide eyes and wrinkled brows. The nurse grabbed one of my arms. The attendant grabbed my other arm. They looked at Shirley. "You'll have to leave. You have to leave," they insisted as they waved her out.

I turned my head as they led me away. "Get the fuck...out...of here, Shirley," I screamed. They led me back toward my area, back toward my room. I was surrounded by other male attendants and nurses. I marched to their pace. I did not resist.

"Who's taking care of the sick people?" I calmly asked.

I was put in my room. "You'll have to stay here," the nurse holding my arm warned. They closed and locked the door, and I sat on the cot. I felt the color returning to my face. I sighed, took a deep breath and lay down with my head on the pillow, covering my forehead with my right arm. I smiled. I felt good about the second punch I had just delivered.

I lay in total contentment for hours and hours. Then the door loudly burst open. In came police officers, male attendants, a nurse, and two uniformed ambulance men carrying a stretcher.

"Stand up and empty everything in your pockets and give it to the nurse," an officer ordered harshly. I had nothing; they'd already taken it all away. "Now lie down on the stretcher."

What the fuck is going on? I wondered. I lay down on the stretcher, which was then raised and held at both ends. I was tightly strapped down and whisked away into a white ambulance, its motor running as it waited outside in the cool late afternoon showers. I could see, as I lowered my chin and head, the ambulance driver signing papers and receiving a large brown manila envelope from a nurse. The uniformed attendant stooped and entered the ambulance and sat on a jump seat next to my side. The rear door was slammed shut and we sped away.

"Where are we going?" I asked.

"Just relax," the attendant said. He lit a cigarette.

"Can I have a drag?"

"Sure." He held the cigarette to my mouth and I inhaled deeply. I felt like a captured dragon as I watched smoke pour from my mouth and nostrils.

"Thanks...Can't you tell me where we're going?" I calmly asked.

"No...not now."

The siren pitched high and low and I felt the speed as we drove. Soon I could hear the flow of traffic and the swoosh of the rain...and I knew we were on the expressway.

He held the cigarette to my mouth again without my asking. I took another deep drag and thought, where the hell are they taking me now?

"Are you sure you can't tell me?" I asked again.

He looked at me and slowly said, "Cook County Hospital." Holy shit, I thought, I've just been KO'd.

I closed my eyes. They became watery but I was too stunned to let the tears flow and cry. I just lay in disbelief ...this is crazy, crazy, crazy, I thought I didn't do anything wrong. My throat became all choked up and I swallowed hard. I opened my wet eyes and lay still, staring at the ceiling of the ambulance, as I remained silent and motionless, swallowing hard for the rest of the ride.

The noise of the mechanical siren lessened as I felt the slowing of the ambulance.

A few turns, a stop and then reverse and the ignition was turned off. The back door opened. I was carried out and transferred from the stretcher onto a gurney, strapped down and wheeled into a building. I didn't look...I just stared up; I had no spirit. I just swallowed hard. I felt the movement and saw the ceiling as I floated through a long corridor and was left alone, still tightly strapped to the gurney. I sighed deeply. I moved my head to the right and then to the left. Just me at the end of a dimly lit hall. I heard voices over a partition in a room nearby. Was that Marty? Was that Sandy? I couldn't be sure. Just solemn male and female voices. The only word of the conversation I could distinguish was the word "he"...was that me? I wondered why no one would talk to me...those voices, is that Sandy and Marty, I wondered again. I lay for twenty minutes or more. My gurney was being rolled. I heard an elevator door open and close. I felt the lift, I was going up, up and then, a sudden noisy stop. The elevator door opened and I was rolled out. The straps were removed and I was told to stand by two black male attendants in white uniforms. I stood. I did not speak. They held my hand as I watched one open a thick door with his key. I entered a large room filled with many men. I was given my labeled name tag to put on my shirt.

"You can walk around or sit down," the attendant said as he walked away. I walked around the room twice, looking and looking, and then I sat down on a folding chair.

"All right, two lines to the right," a female nurse yelled. Everyone obeyed. I stood in a line. As I moved forward to the nurse's aide at the front of my line, she handed me two tiny cups, one containing two pills and one with water. I just stood still.

"Hurry, hurry, you have to take them in front of me," she said.

I swallowed the pills and handed back the empty cups to the outstretched hand of one of the inmates who assisted. I was officially institutionalized. I was no longer me. I had no ego. I had no pride. All I felt was shame, and I didn't cry.

Everyone was asked to leave the large room, and I followed the crowd there to the door on my right. I entered the men's psycho ward of Cook County Hospital Mental Health Clinic. It was another large room, occupied by an assortment of men of all different ages, from the twenties on up. There weren't enough chairs for all who were there, so I sat on the floor with my back against the white wall. People were smoking. They were asking orderlies for lights. I had no cigarettes. I saw a young man standing alone. I got up and asked if I could have a cigarette. He handed me one and without saying a word, I nodded my thanks. I walked to an orderly and got a light. I enjoyed that first puff and more. When the cigarette had almost burned out, I went to another man and asked for one, without a voice but with just the look of my eyes. He handed me a cigarette and I lit the second from the first. This went on for hours as I scouted the room and walked around picking out men who I saw or thought had cigarettes; then with my eyes, a nod of the head, a motion of my hand, or perhaps a whisper, I would ask for a cigarette. Some looked away, some walked away. Occasionally, I went dry before finding a friend with a cigarette and had to get a fresh light from an orderly. Sometimes those who I thought were friends would walk away as I approached. It's their cigarettes and I was no longer a friend, they must have thought! There were people talking; it was not all silence. But there were those who did and those who didn't. That first day, I was one of those who didn't.

An orderly stood at the door. "Dinner, dinner, dinner," he announced. I followed the crowd and the sounds of shuffling shoes. The large room I had been in before was now the dining room. The rows of long tables were not assigned. You just sat where you could. We were served our trays as we sat. I found a place and sat, only a spoon and napkin in front of me. Where's my knife and fork, I thought I looked to my right, I looked to my left, to my front and down the row. All anyone had was a tablespoon. I wondered why! Many men were talking in normal tones, but I didn't want to break my silence above a whisper. I looked to my right. "Why is there only a spoon?" I whispered.

His one eye glanced at my eye. He shrugged his shoulder and looked ahead as he quickly ate. I waited, fearing someone would hear and think me foolish.

I looked at the man on my left. "Why is there only a spoon?" I whispered.

He did not acknowledge me. I'll never know, I thought, as I ate in silence with my spoon.

After dinner, we returned to the ward. I found an empty chair and just sat and watched all the men. I just want to get out of here, I just want to go home...I'm going to go crazy if I stay here. An orderly was loudly ordering a man, about twenty-five, to go sit down...soon there were three other orderlies at his side. The inmate started to shout cuss words against his mother and threatened to kill her when he got out. The men in the white shirts gave him one final order to sit down and be quiet. The inmate just raised his voice louder and louder. Two more orderlies arrived. They grabbed him from all sides and carried him out screaming through a door and down a hall. Eventually, the screams stopped. The man next to me said, "He's had it."

"Yeah," I said. "What will they do?"

"They'll put him in a straitjacket and strap him to a bed in a small room for the night. He'll be quiet tomorrow."

"How do you know?"

"It happens all the time."

He got up and left. Hey, I talked to someone who seemed normal, I thought. But what the hell is he doing here, I wondered.

I walked up to an orderly. "How long do I have to stay here?" I asked softly. He looked at me.

"When did you get here?"

"Today."

"Eight more days."

"Eight more days," I repeated, "then I can go home."

"That depends on the psychiatrist," he answered. "Didn't you get a form explaining everything? Over there on the table are forms. Take one and read it."

I walked over to the card table in the corner that held a stack of long three-fold forms. I picked up one and sat in a comer and read:

LEGAL RIGHTS AND PROCEDURES FOR PATIENTS IN THE MENTAL HEALTH CLINIC

1. THE REASON FOR YOUR DETENTION IN THE CLINIC

You are presently in the Cook County Mental Health Clinic because a petition and doctor's certificate have been filed which state that you are mentally ill or a person in need of mental treatment requiring hospital care. It is your right to have a complete hearing on the petition before the Circuit Court of Cook County, County Division.

2. YOUR RIGHTS TO ANY ATTORNEY

You may hire a private attorney to represent you at the court hearing. However, if you do not have the funds to hire an attorney, the Public Defender will represent you at your request or demand. The Public Defender interviews patients in the ward and you can see him then or advise your social worker beforehand that you are requesting the Public Defender because you cannot pay for the services of an attorney.

3. HOW YOUR CASE WILL BE HANDLED

Within three days after you enter the Clinic you will be examined by a commission of two psychiatrists. Seven days after you enter the Clinic, your case will come up for hearing before the Circuit Court of Cook County, County Division sitting in the Clinic.

Warning! If you are charged with a crime, any admissions you make at this hearing may be used against you.

(a) You May Demand A Trial by Jury .

At any time prior to your hearing, you or your attorney may demand a trial by jury to determine your mental condition. If a jury demand is made, the hearing will end and you will be returned to your ward to await jury trial.

(b) You May Allow Your case to be Decided by the Judge.

If no jury demand is made, the judge hears your testimony and the testimony of witnesses in your case. In addition he will study the report of the commission of psychiatrists who examined you, and he will also consult with your ward psychiatrist. On the basis of this evidence the judge arrives at a decision in regard to your mental condition.

4. HOW YOUR CASE MAY BE DISPOSED OF.

After a trial by jury or a hearing by the Court sitting without a jury, the judge will enter one of the following orders:

1. That the Petition be dismissed and that you be discharged from custody. (If you are under arrest, you will be returned to the police.)

2. That you be committed to a mental hospital as a person who is mentally ill or in need of mental treatment. In the event that it is determined that you are mentally ill, then you lose your civil rights.

3. That you be committed to the care and custody of relatives as a person who is mentally ill or in need of mental treatment. If it is determined that you are mentally ill, then you lose your civil rights.

Holy shit, I thought, this place is like a prison. I don't belong here; I have no control over my own fate. Eight more days before a hearing. I'll go crazy here. I was bumming cigarettes like a crazy man. I was looking at spoons like a crazy man. Soon, I thought, I'll be like the men walking around here and talking to themselves if I don't get out. I was beginning to question my own sanity. I reread and reread the form, the next to-the-bottom paragraph ..."committed to a mental hospital," for how long, I wondered ...forever? No civil rights. How did this ever happen? I began to reflect. Nothing made sense. I thought about Sandy...I wasn't angry, I was mellow and confused. I was ashamed of the secrets and lies I had told Shirley about Sandy. That wasn't like me at all. I was really depressed over that; I was depressed by the whole situation. I felt my throat choke and I swallowed. I sat on the floor thinking of Sandy. I couldn't get her out of my mind. I just remained mellow and depressed in my thoughts.

Later, everyone lined up for pills. I swallowed mine and sat back down on the floor, staring at everyone in the room. This place is a snake pit, I thought. After a while, the lights flashed on and off twice.

"Bedtime, bedtime," the orderlies shouted.

I followed the crowd into a very large room. Cots were lined up side by side. I didn't know where to go. I stood by the door.

An orderly came over to me; he looked at my name tag and then at his clipboard. He lifted the sheets of paper, looking for my name.

"Follow me," he said.

He showed me my cot. I lay down with my right arm over my forehead. The lights were turned low. I couldn't sleep; I just lay on my back, looking at the ceiling, lost in my thoughts. The snoring started. How do you sleep in this place, I wondered. I closed my eyes; my thoughts drowned out the noise. I felt my wrist grasped lightly. I opened my eyes. It was a black orderly. "Are you Sherwin-?" He pronounced my last name correctly.

"Yes," I said.

"Your wife's on the phone," he said softly. "Do you want to talk to her?"

"Sure," I answered calmly.

I followed him out of the room through a door at the end to a small office. He nodded for me to pick up the phone receiver lying on the desk. "Just a few minutes," he said as he left

I picked up the receiver. "Hello," I said solemnly.

"Hi," the mellow voice answered. "How are you doing?"

"How am I supposed to be doing?"

"Are you OK?"

I paused. "Sandy, you have to get me out of here."

"I know, I know ...I want you home. " I felt her tears.

"Sandy...you have to get me out of here," I softly repeated.

"I'll try, I'll try tomorrow ...I promise, I'll try. I'll do everything possible." I felt her tears more.

"Is there anything you need?" she asked.

"Cigarettes."

"I'll get them there somehow," she said. "Who all knows about this?" I asked.

"Nobody knows except your cousins...and Melvin."

"I don't want my folks to know. I don't want them to ever know."

"I know. They won't," she promised. "I miss you, I miss you." I paused.

"I miss you too," I said.

The orderly came in and motioned for me to hang up.

"I have to hang up...the orderly wants me off the phone."

"I'll try my best tomorrow, I promise. I love you."

"Me too...I gotta go. Good-bye." I slowly put the receiver back down.

"I can get in trouble for doing this," the orderly said.

"I know, I appreciate that...Do you mind if I ask you a question?"

"What?" the orderly asked cautiously.

"Why do they only have spoons?"

"What?"

"Why do they only have spoons in the dining area?"

"They don't allow anyone to have a fork or knife...it could be dangerous." He laughed.

"Thanks." I felt foolish and stupid as I followed him back to my bed. I hope he doesn't put that in his report, I thought.

I lay on my back and thought of Sandy. She'll get me out tomorrow. I know Sandy, she'll get me out tomorrow ...and then I can go home. With those thoughts I fell asleep.

The next morning, we were awakened early. I went to the toilet and followed everyone back out to the ward. We were given our pills and then had breakfast in the dining room. Soon it will be nine o'clock and Sandy will be working on getting me out. I was nervously confident that I would be freed.

More pills and then lunch, and still no word. It was approaching five o'clock. I was losing confidence; then an orderly shouted out my name. I rushed over to him. He looked at my tag. "I have a package for you." He handed me a brown bag. It contained a carton of Salems and a note:

149

Honey,
I can't do anything. I really tried. You have to wait for
your hearing another seven days. Marty is dropping off
cigarettes. I love you very much.
Sandy

I took a deep breath. I knew Sandy had tried. I looked around the ward. I didn't know how I was going to put up with this shit for another seven, or was it another eight, days. I didn't know. I was really, really depressed.

That evening was social hour in the dining room. The tables were cleared and music from a phonograph was playing as we entered. The door on the opposite end opened and female inmates wearing blue dresses entered. I sat down in one of the chairs lined up against the wall. The female social director announced that we should all find a partner and dance. I watched as couples started to fill the center floor and dance, some cheek to cheek. This is stupid, I thought. I wouldn't even fuck one of these crazy broads. They all looked weird to me. But then, I thought, maybe I look weird to them too. Everyone was dancing or walking around, and I was the only one sitting. An orderly came over to my chair.

"Aren't you going to dance?" he pleasantly asked.

I looked up. "Sure," I answered as I stood up. He'll put on my report that I'm antisocial if I don't dance, I thought. I found a woman standing nearby.

"Would you like to dance?" I asked.

Please say no, I prayed. She nodded yes. We walked to the center of the floor. I placed my right hand on her waist and held my left hand high. She placed her right hand in mine. We danced six inches apart.

"Do you come here often?" I asked.

She shook her head no. My sense of humor was coming back. I accepted the fact that I'd be here for another eight days

150

at most. I danced us by the orderly who had suggested that I dance. He saw me; I smiled...I hoped he was giving me a good report. I danced another time with someone else. I walked around. I stood and had punch by the table in a corner. Finally, the party was over and all the men and women went through their separate doors back to the wards. We had our pills and went to bed.

One afternoon several days later, tables and chairs were placed near the rear of the ward. On one side of the tables sat two psychiatrists to talk to the persons whose names were being read aloud by an orderly. My name was called and I stood in line. After a while, I sat down facing the black psychiatrist; at his side sat a white psychiatrist. Both were wearing suits. The black psychiatrist studied my file. He looked up. "Do you know why you're here?" he asked.

"No," I answered.

"No?" His voice was raised loudly. "It says here that you're paranoid schizophrenic, homicidal, suicidal, and delusional." His tone was stern. He looked at my face, awaiting my answer.

I was taken aback. I couldn't believe what I had just heard. I paused before I answered, very cautious in my choice of words. I was scared.

"I'm not suicidal."

"Then why are you here?" he asked authoritatively.

"I was taking a drug, Methedrine...and apparently it caused me to hallucinate," I said calmly.

His eyes fell back to the report. "Hmm, yes...I see Methedrine here. OK, that's all. Next..."

I got up and watched both psychiatrists write on their file as I left.

Holy shit, I thought. Paranoid schizophrenic, where the fuck did they get that?

Homicidal? I had threatened to kill Sandy...but those were just words of anger. I never would have hurt her.

Suicidal?...that's crazy. Delusional?...that fucking dinosaur. I never should have told Stein. I looked back, wondering what they had written in that report. I was nervously depressed. I was worried. I hoped my choice of words had been right. I didn't know. I was afraid to say anything else. I was afraid to speak up and defend myself. I would probably sound like a crazy man saying he's sane. My life was in their hands. They could have me put away for a long, long, time, I thought.

Shit!

The time passed slowly...the days took forever. I ran out of cigarettes. I was bumming again. I was all alone. I heard from no one.

Finally, the next day was my hearing date. I barely slept that night. I had barely slept the previous nights...I was just worried ...constantly worrying.

I had breakfast, I had pills...and finally in the ward, two orderlies called out names to form a line by the door. My name was called, and I stood in line.

They checked our tags and ticked our names off their lists. "Follow us," they said.

We all stood in the huge elevator and rode down together. The elevator door noisily opened, and we followed the orderlies as we disembarked in a corridor. One of them knocked on the solid steel door and a bailiff answered. They stood together, the bailiff and the two orderlies, exchanging papers, and then the door closed and the bailiff was gone.

I imagined a judge in a black robe sitting high on his bench. I imagined a witness chair, a cub reporter and the bailiff ...All those things beyond the door, I imagined. I was nervous. I was scared. I hope they call me first, I thought.

After what seemed to be a long, long, time, I heard the sound of the door. The bailiff called a name. It wasn't mine. After a while, the sound of the door, the inmate returned ...he was not smiling. Another name was called. It was not mine.

"How did it go?" I whispered.

"I don't know," he replied. That's all that was said. He sat on the floor. I thought about what could happen to me if they didn't set me free. I thought about the state mental hospital and how they would get me there, and how they would keep me there for thirty days or more. My stomach ached, my arms felt tight and I prayed...I was scared. This went on for over an hour and then my name was called.

The bailiff escorted me through the door into the hearing room. There was no judge in a black robe sitting high on his bench. Instead, there was a mahogany conference table with three men on one side, and empty chairs in front of them. There was a court reporter. Everyone was busy reading files. I saw Sandy, and the bailiff let me sit next to her. Sandy smiled; she squeezed my arm. I nodded hello and I sat still. I sat for five minutes and then the man sitting in the center of the conference table called my name.

The bailiff led me to the chair in front of the man he called your honor. He read my file and then looked at me.

"Do you expect to go home?"

"I hope so, your honor."

"It says here that they had trouble with you at Forest Hospital in Des Plaines." I nodded yes.

"Speak up."

"Yes, your honor."

"You were not following Dr. Stein's orders."

"No, your honor."

"Why?"

"I didn't want to see him any more."

"Your wife promised the court if we release you that you would see a different psychiatrist. Will you do that?"

"Yes, your honor."

He asked the bailiff to call my wife. Sandy came forward and sat in the empty chair next to me.

"Have you already made arrangements for your husband to see a psychiatrist?"

"Yes, your honor," Sandy answered. "Who?"

"Dr. Jordan Scher, your honor," Sandy answered.

"Do you feel comfortable about your husband coming home?"

"Yes, your honor."

"OK...That's all...We will decide."

Sandy and I stood up. She smiled and squeezed my hand as the bailiff led me away. I sat on the floor next to the other inmates back in the corridor behind the locked door. I felt fairly confident I would be set free, but I wasn't really sure. I was still very nervous.

All the other patients and inmates now had been seen. We all sat and stood to hear who would go home and who would go to the state hospital or to jail. It seemed like an eternity and then I heard the sound of the door. The bailiff handed an orderly a list of names.

"All right, the following names are going to go home," the orderly announced. My name was the third one called. There were two others. That was all. "You five can follow the bailiff out," the orderly said, handing us each a bag containing the personal belongings that had been taken from us when we were admitted. "The others stay with me."

I was able to breathe again as I waited for the bailiff to lead us out. Several of the seven men who were not being released broke down and cried. One wailed as you would at a funeral.

I gave the wailing man a final look, and I followed the bailiff out. That wailing man could have been me, I thought. The door closed and the bailiff pointed past the empty hearing room to the exit in the rear.

"Just go out that door. Your families are there," he said.

We filed out into the corridor. Sandy was there. She ran into my arms. We hugged very tightly; we kissed. She had tears in her eyes; I did not. Marty came over to me and gave me a hug. I hugged him back. It felt good to be free. We walked together through the corridor.

"Dr. Scher has time this afternoon and I'm to call and let him know if you were released. We'll stop for lunch first and I'll make the call."

"OK," I said, "but what's that all about?"

"I made a lot of calls while you were gone and I was told by one of the psychiatrists here that your chances of being released would be better if I arranged for a doctor to see you when you got out."

"Fine," I answered. "Who is he and how did you get ahold of him?"

"He's on the Irv Kupcinet talk show often...he's in the gossip column all the time. And he's supposed to be very good, so I called."

"OK," I answered.

"Marty will drop us off after lunch, and then we can take a cab home. His office is on the Near North Side."

"OK," I said,

"My mother is in town and staying with us for a few days. Is that OK?"

"Sandy, I always enjoy your mother. Of course it's OK."

I talked to Marty. He told me my folks thought I was out of town. "Deanie, Shirley, Sydney always ask about you," he said.

Sandy and I held and squeezed hands as Marty drove us to a small restaurant on the Near North Side. I had always loved Chicago's Gold Coast on the Near North Side. But this time I saw beauty in the freedom people had as we drove through neighborhoods that were not as nice.

Sandy made the call and returned to the table. "He wants to see us both at one," she said. "Both?" I asked.

"That's what he said."

Marty looked at his watch, "The timing is perfect...by the time we finish lunch and I drop you off, it will be one."

Marty dropped us off in front of a two-story brownstone building, Dr. Scher's office and residence. He handed me a paper.

"Sherwin, here's the receipt for your personal belongings I got when you checked in. Make sure you have everything."

"Thanks." I put the green paper in my pocket. It listed a wristwatch, a wallet with two dollars in it, and a green pen. "I'll look at it later." So that had been Marty's voice I'd heard when I was brought by ambulance to the hospital, I thought. I wondered if I'd heard Sandy's voice too, as I lay strapped to a gurney, no one talking to me.

We walked into the building, to the receptionist's desk. She knew who we were and said she would tell Dr. Scher we had arrived.

We entered his private office. It had a very homey, comfortable feel. He was a tall man, about six foot two. He shook my hand and Sandy's, too. We sat in front of his desk.

"So how does it feel to be out? Pretty good?" He smiled.

"Yes," I answered.

"So tell me what happened with you and this Dr. Stein."

I told him about the ambulance coming to my house, about my raised voice on the phone with Stein, the two cups of coffee and the police. I told him that Cook County Hospital had me diagnosed as paranoid schizophrenic from Stein. He laughed. "It sounds like Stein was the paranoid schizophrenic."

I smiled. It made me feel good, even though I knew that was what he was trying to do.

He started to direct his questions at Sandy. He put her on the defensive a few times. I could see that she felt uncomfortable. I like this man, I thought. He told me he would like to see me tomorrow and then three times a week to start.

"Sandy, too?" I asked. "No, just you."

"Fine," I said.

We took a cab home. We talked about the office.

"Everything is fine, and everyone thinks you were out of town," Sandy said.

"I'll go in tomorrow morning and drive you there too," I answered.

Sandy squeezed my hand and I gently squeezed back. When we arrived, I got out my wallet with the two dollars, which had been returned to me. Sandy laughed and paid the bill. I laughed too. She opened the door and we went into our apartment. My mother-in-law stood in the living room.

"Hi," I said. I walked over to her. We hugged tightly. I felt the sincerity of her long embrace. I wouldn't let her go now that we had hugged so long. I didn't want her to see the watering of my eyes. Finally, I was back in control and released her from our embrace. She didn't see my watery eyes but I saw her silent tears. I looked around the room. Gosh, it's good to be home, I thought.

"What did you do to the windows?" I asked.

My mother-in-law laughed. "I heard all about your ghost pictures and Becky and I washed all the windows so hard...all you'll be able to see is outside."

I laughed, too. "Does Becky know about the pictures?"

"No..." Sandy and my mother-in-law said, "she'd quit working here if she knew." We all laughed.

"Where's Matthew?" I asked.

"In the playpen in the dining room," Sandy said.

I walked in alone. "Hi, big fellow," I said. I picked him up and gave him a big hug and kiss, my eyes watering. Gosh, it was great to be home.

I had a great home-cooked meal. We ate and talked in the dining room. I was the first to go to bed. I was so tired, I just went right to sleep.

Sandy and I arrived early at the office the next morning. Marshall and the three girls were there. Everyone was glad to see me. Sandy said Marshall didn't know, but I could tell he did. My desk was clean except for a few things only I could do. My first call was from the Exchange National Bank.

"Sherwin...this is Ted."

"Hi, Ted," I said.

"I was on vacation, and I just got back and your letter was on my desk. You want Marshall's name off the account?" he asked.

Oh, my God, I thought. I'd forgotten all about that.

"No, Ted. Leave the name on and just mail back the letter to my personal attention.

Give me a call when you're clear. We'll have lunch."

"Great, Sherwin. I'll call you next week."

So they had mailed that letter. I smiled.

I called my folks and talked to my mother. I told her I was back in town and would see them Sunday.

I was studying the production reports, and I told everyone that when the salesmen called in, I wanted to talk to them. It was as if I'd never left.

Late that afternoon, I went to see Dr. Scher. We talked a lot about Methedrine. He knew all about the drug. Many of his patients were hard-drug addicts. And he was prescribing Methadone (not to be confused with Methedrine) as a substitute for heroin.

"Are they staying off heroin?" I asked.

"Some do...some don't," he answered.

"Are you going to prescribe medication for me?" I asked. "Why?"

"Well, Stein said I needed it."

"You don't need any medication," he answered.

That whole argument with Sandy had started with my throwing away my pills. I kept that thought to myself.

158

As I drove home, I thought about suing Stein. But the only attorney I would use would be Melvin, who was basically a divorce and real estate attorney. I had never needed his services. I figured he hadn't come to my rescue because Deanie and Shirley had probably told him how sick I was and that he would be doing a disservice. I'll find out the truth one day, I thought. I decided not to sue Stein. I might not win. The attorney I used specialized in insurance law and I was too ashamed of what had happened to tell my story to him or to any other attorney he might recommend.

I went home. I looked at my mail. There was a manila envelope from Dr. Rhine.

That's right, I had sent him some photos, I remembered. I read the letter.

May 14, 1964

Dear Mr. Ernst:

I have received and am now returning the material you sent me, involving the photographic effects.

From such examination as I have been able to give them I do not take these to be of interest to the research field in which I am engaged. I would recommend a shift of interest so long as there is any slightest question about your health. When that stage is happily past, I should be glad to hear from you again if your interests warrant it.

All good wishes for your progress.

Sincerely yours,
J.B. Rhine

"Holy shit," I thought. I really had made a total ass out of myself. I never should have sent him those pictures. They weren't that good. And that letter I let Stein write. I'm sure

Stein must have explained that I was his patient and implied I was delusional. God, could I kick myself. "Damn it, damn it, damn it." I muttered as I gritted my teeth. If I suffered from any delusion, it was the delusion that Stein had considered our relationship anything other than a doctor/patient relationship. I was angry and depressed all at once. I went to bed before Sandy and her mother again that night, tossing and turning and trying to force myself to go to sleep. I couldn't. I thought about the stretcher and being strapped in and about the attendant telling me I was going to Cook County Hospital; I thought about being scared to death as I waited for the verdict of my hearing; I thought about everything else I could think about. I sat up in bed, turned on the light and lit a cigarette. "Whew," I thought as I finished my cigarette and finally went to sleep.

The next morning, I didn't go to the office. I had told Sandy I wouldn't be in and that I would be out selling, but I just didn't feel like selling myself to anyone, so I hung out at a restaurant, drinking coffee. Later, I went to my afternoon appointment with Scher. I sat across from his desk and smoked a cigarette while he smoked his pipe. I remained silent, just puffing on my cigarette. He remained silent, smoking his pipe. I reached my hand over his desk to put out my cigarette. Our eyes made contact. My eyes reddened, the tear ducts swelled, my cheeks puffed. I put my face in my palms and I bawled like a baby. I couldn't stop. I just bawled and bawled. I pulled out my handkerchief and wiped my eyes and my face.

"I don't believe I'm doing this...I don't believe I'm doing this," I said as I started to wipe my eyes and running nose. I was regaining my composure and sat up straight.

"I don't believe I did that," I said as I wiped away the rest of the tears. I had my composure back. "You know what's so incredible, Dr. Scher?" I asked with my nose still full.

"What?"

"That's the first time in my life I've ever cried in front of a man."

He remained silent.

"I'm OK now...Do you mind if l leave?" "No. You can leave if you want." "Thanks. I'll see you tomorrow."

I drove home. There was a package from Cook County Hospital addressed to me. Inside was another package from Dr. Stein. Apparently, it had reached there after I had left. I opened the package. It was a letter and a book.

SAM I. STEIN, M.D., Ph.D.
ABRAHAM LINCOLN RESEARCH INSTITUTE
AND MEDICAL CENTER
4535 OAKTON STREET • SKOKIE, ILLINOIS

MAY 13, 1964

Mr. Sherwin Ernst
711 Montrose Avenue
Chicago 13, Illinois

Dear Sherman,
If you are sane as you insist, you will recognize

(1) that your wife and I have sincere attitudes and intentions regarding you (I did not keep the money for your missed appointment, and I am not charging a fee for many hours of service over these several days),

(2) that misunderstandings, even of significant scope, can yet develop in the field of mental health,

(3) that you should stop hating those of us who have been trying to be helpful to you, and instead make the most of your current experience by observing what are the defects in our present methods, and also what you can do to help institute such corrective measures as are

necessary to make the mental health situation more objective, as did Mr. Clifford Beers in his book entitled THE MIND THAT FOUND ITSELF, when he found himself in an experience comparable to yours. You are liked by all who meet you.

Sincerely,
Sam I. Stein, M.D.

I skimmed the book. It was about a man who kept going in and out of mental institutions all his life until he finally found himself. I just didn't understand how Stein could see any similarities between that man and me. I shook my head. That fucking Stein just doesn't get it, I thought I had never questioned his sincere attitude or intentions regarding me. He just had never known me as a patient. He never asked what had happened. He just assumed Sandy was telling the truth. He had never bothered to find out that it was she, not me, who was the violent one, the one who always started the fights. You're damn right I hate you, you bastard. You took away my freedom. You took away my life. I was really glad I hadn't gotten that book yesterday. And then I laughed as I reread the letter. His secretary had gotten my first name wrong.

Late that night, Sandy and I had sex. She was tense; I was not. I wasn't a lover; I was just a fuck. That wasn't like me nor was that like her. But I felt good. I had gotten a lot out of my system that day and that night too.

My mother-in-law returned to Denver. Deanie, Shirley, Marty and Sydney came over one night just to say hello, and we just spoke briefly about what had happened.

Except for a comment or two about how it had been done for my own good, nothing more was said. I resented those comments of reassurance that it was done for my good. Like I had even the slightest thought that they had done it to punish me. They must really think I was sick. I'm glad my mother never found out. It would have ruined her relationship with Sandy for life. As for Deanie and Shirley, my mother would have really been upset with them no matter what they said. I guess my mother is really the only person in the world who knows me, I thought-even without words. My father would have been very sad, but he would have believed that Deanie and Shirley had done the right thing. Ojeh would have sided with my mother, but she would have still loved Sandy. Onnie and Sam...they would have been confused and just listened and not taken sides. I'm sure glad they never knew. I saw them that Sunday; all the Wicker Park family were at my folks' house.

I had asked Sandy where she and Matthew were when the ambulance came that day. They were upstairs in Bobbie's apartment. I had seen Bobbie several times since I'd been back. One day she stopped me in the hallway.

"Sherwin, are you mad at me?" she asked.

"No, why?"

"I don't know...you act upset when we talk."

"No," I answered.

"Sherwin, I told Sandy that day she should not call the ambulance. If you guys are fighting, I told her she should just leave."

I looked at Bobbie.

"Thanks, Bobbie, I appreciate that"

She's only twenty-one and she's smarter than all of them, I thought. She kissed me on the cheek and ran upstairs.

This whole thing was festering within me. I didn't want a confrontation with Sandy, but I did want to discuss it. Sandy swore that she'd never signed any papers and that it was all Stein's suggestion, which he said was for my good.

I wanted to hear more than that Stein had recommended it...I wanted to hear why Sandy and my cousins didn't talk to me first. But most importantly, I wanted to know why Sandy didn't stand by her man and say she had provoked the fight and struck out at me first all those times. Especially the last time. How could she take an order from Stein that would do her man harm? I would never accept what she had done. But at least she should ask for my forgiveness and tell Deanie, Shirley, Marty and Sydney they were all wrong. Say that, I thought, let me digest that, and we can get on with our lives...but not before.

I saw the humor in several of the incidents. I could find the humor in the crazy wagon at my front door. I could find the humor in my shouts of anger at Shirley. I thought my bumming cigarettes and wondering about the spoons was hilarious and much more. I shared those types of experiences with Sandy in a laughing and desperately humorous manner. It didn't work. Just the opposite. She became furious with my making light of those things. She would display fits of anger. I reacted to her anger. "Fuck you ...go call Stein," I'd say as I stormed out of the room. I'd get angry thinking about that motherfucker. It's just going to take one more bullshit thing with Sandy and I'm going to sue that bastard. Any angry word Sandy used I would rebut with Stein's name. It reached the point where it would just take the wrong choice of word or the wrong tone of voice to ignite the spark of anger in either one of us.

After one of these arguments, I stormed out the front door. She caught my sleeve. "Where are you going?" she demanded.

"Get your fucking hand off my shirt or this time you're really going to end up on the floor," I snarled.

She released her hold.

"Why don't you just call Stein, or, better still, call Scher? Then we'll see who's the one that belongs in the hospital." With those words I left and drove to the Near North Side. My anger had turned to depression by the time I'd parked the car. I can't live like this. I just can't go on like this, I thought. I dialed from a pay phone and waited for its second ring. It was always the second ring if she was home.

"Hello." the low voice answered.

"Geri?"

"Sherwin!" The voice brightened.

"Can I come over?"

"Sure."

"I'll be there in a few minutes. I'm down the street at a payphone."

I knocked twice. Geri looked the same. The dimly lighted apartment was the same. Nothing had changed. We sat on the floor. I knew Geri had been a heroin addict in New York. I knew she had gotten off it, but I felt she had contacts in Chicago and that she could get heroin. I'd never had it before. but I knew if anything could make me forget, forget what had happened, it would be heroin. not Methedrine. I looked into her eyes; it was the first time she had ever seen me serious. I could tell she sensed something different about me as she awaited my words. "Geri, can you do me a big favor?" I asked.

"What, Sherwin?" she innocently answered.

"Can you get me some heroin?" I slowly got the words out of my mouth.

I had struck a core in her that brought fright to her face as she shook her head.

"No...absolutely no. I don't use that stuff any more. I don't want to go back."

"Not for you. It's for me."

"I understand," she said, "but I won't even associate with those people any more."

I felt that the core I had struck was the fear of her own weakness for the drug. I felt bad that I had raised that temptation.

"OK...I'll never ask again."

"Please don't, Sherwin."

"Can I have some Meth?"

"Sure," the old Geri answered.

We both had a pop in the arm. I waited for its effect. Then I told my story. My way, the funny way. At first she was very upset with Sandy, but then I got her laughing. I also told her about the pictures, the *Zadik*, the other dimension. Geri said I was taking too much Methedrine and I was hallucinating; I was off the wall. I was disappointed that Geri didn't believe me either. I dropped the subject. I knew what was hallucination and what was real. I had just that one pop and went home. Sandy was reading in bed. We didn't say a word. I got undressed and put my head on her lap as I lay next to her.

She rubbed my head. One minute I was angry and storming out of the apartment. And now, I was back in a mellow, loving mood. Maybe I am crazy, I thought. We kissed very passionately. We had sex. It was great.

The next day, I refilled my prescription, and I was secretly back on Methedrine. I was working long, hard hours, my sex life returned, I was seeing Scher just once a week, and he didn't know I was taking Meth. He had moved his office to the Marina Twin Towers near the Chicago River. It was my first visit to his new location. Today I was going to tell him I didn't want to see him any more, and that everything between Sandy and me was fine.

The Marina Tower buildings are two 61-floor cylindrical complexes whose first 19 floors are parking. I hadn't even known there were offices there; I thought it was just apartments. I held a slip of paper in my hand with Scher's name and suite number. I got off the elevator into the deserted corridor, looking for his office. I walked and walked and walked. This is the longest fucking hallway I've ever been in, I thought. After a while, I started to panic. I've always been to appointments on time; it was my nature.

That's why I'd always hated going places with Sandy. She was always late.

I had to stop and catch my breath and wipe my brow. This is ridiculous, I thought.

I must have passed it. I turned and walked in the opposite direction. None of these suites had names on their doors- just numbers. That's what I did, I thought, I missed the number. Or am I in the wrong building? No...I'm very, very careful with appointments. I just missed the number, I thought as I walked and walked and walked. I couldn't believe I hadn't seen another soul in the corridor all this time. I would have stopped and asked where this number was. All of a sudden I had a flash of insight. *I don't believe I did that. I don't believe I did that*, I chuckled. I've been walking around in a fucking circle all this time. I had forgotten the building was round. I had passed the room dozens of times. Why hadn't I seen it? I didn't know, but now I'd found it. I straightened my tie, wiped my brow and I looked at my watch. I was twenty-five minutes late. I sheepishly entered the room. The receptionist looked up.

"I'm sorry, Dr. Scher had an emergency. I tried calling you at your office but you had already left. Can you come back Friday at this time?"

"Sure," I answered. I was glad he wasn't there. I knew he might have sensed I was on Meth because of my sweat from all that walking.

I grabbed a cab and went back to the office. I decided to stop taking the drug for a while.

Four days later, I saw Scher and told him I didn't want to see him any more. I was curious as to what he would say. He shrugged. "OK," he said. He was not upset.

"Dr. Scher," I asked, "if you were my doctor instead of Stein, and my wife called and told you I was violent and had thrown away my pills...what would you have done? How would you have diagnosed me?"

"Sherwin, you developed a model psychosis from Methedrine. I would have told Sandy to leave you, that's all."

"And what about those spirit pictures, the *Zadik*, the other dimension, the dinosaur, and all those other things?"

"Sherwin, you were hallucinating," he answered.

I stood up and shook his hand. I thanked him and told him I had enjoyed our visits. "One last thing before I leave," I paused at the door and looked at Dr. Scher. "The dinosaur was a hallucination ...or who knows, maybe I did have a vision, I'll never know. The pictures Sandy and I saw together could have been *folie a deux,* and a lot of the other things were hallucinations," I agreed, "but that man across the yard, the *Zadik*, my other me and the *Zadik* in that chamber, and my anima on the window, those were real, Dr. Scher." I smiled and left.

I felt really good when I arrived home that evening, that is, until I was greeted at the front door by Sandy. I could tell by her face, the smallness of her eyes, the wrinkles on her brow and the fire in her glare. She looked at my face with anger in her eyes.

"You bastard," she whispered through tight lips. "You bastard," she quickly repeated, "I can't believe you did that" Her voice rose.

"What's the big deal? So I quit seeing Dr. Scher, so what, and besides, how did you find out?" I demanded.

Her mouth opened, a look of disbelief on her face. "You what?" she screamed. "You what?"

"I quit seeing Scher. What are you screaming about?"

She pointed to the bedroom. I walked to the doorway and looked. On the bed was my Methedrine.

"Fuck you, I'm leaving," I said. "And don't try and stop me because you ain't going to."

I got my suitcase and packed.

"Go ahead...Go. Go. Go....I don't want you. Go!" she shouted.

I packed my clothes and toiletries quickly. I took my Meth and syringe and needles from the bed. She had found it under my sweaters. And this was summer. That nosy bitch, I thought. I was at the front door with my packed suitcase. I set it down and started to walk to the dining room.

"Where are you going?" she demanded.

"To kiss Matthew goodnight."

"Don't you touch my son...Don't ever touch him. Just get out of my house." I left quickly. Free at last. Thank God, I thought.

I drove to Old Town, bordering on the Near North Side. I hoped Don would still be home, and that he had not yet left to hit the bar scene. Don lived in a coach house; he had a small apartment, one bedroom with two beds. It was a great bachelor's pad. I knew Don would put me up for a while until I could find my own place. Don was with a different broad every night of the week. If he brought anyone back to his place, I would just sleep on the couch, I thought. I parked my car and stood at his door with my suitcase at my side as I knocked. I saw the light and I knew he was home. The door opened.

"Sherwin," he said, looking at my suitcase, "did you and Sandy have a fight?" He chuckled.

"Yeah...Don't ask any questions. Can I stay here for a while until I find an apartment?"

"Sure. Come on in." He pointed to the bedroom. "You can have the end bed...put your stuff away."

"Thanks, Don."

I unpacked and took my shaving kit to the bathroom.

"Sherwin. Don't move any of my pills. They're arranged in a certain order."

"Don, I won't touch your pills."

"Do you want one? I got Methedrine pills too."

"No, you know I really don't like pills."

"That's right. You take liquid Methedrine. I don't see how you use that needle," he chuckled.

Don was a constant chuckler. He invited me to go with him when he hit the late bar scene in three more hours. I accepted his invitation but told him I wasn't interested in picking up any broad. I just wanted a fuckless rest until I got my own place. My taste in women was entirely different from Don's.

I sat in the living room, watching Don get ready. The bathroom door was open. It was unbelievable, the way he dried off after his shower, the way he brushed his teeth and shaved, the way he combed his hair. He didn't wipe himself dry, he patted himself dry. The shave, the hard brushing of his teeth, I thought he'd never finish. The combing of his hair. It was painstaking perfection. No wonder he'd told me three hours. It was going to take three hours for him to dress. I had watched two sitcoms and an hour-long variety show, shaved, showered, brushed my teeth, combed my hair, dressed and was watching the late news. Don was still getting dressed and had already taken three different pills since he started. At exactly three hours, he was at the front door.

"Let's go," he chuckled.

If Don was seeing Scher, he'd still be walking, I thought.

We walked a block to Wells Street, the main street in Old Town. We went to three different bars, all crowded. Don always ordered ginger ale and I had club soda with a lime. Don was well liked; he knew a lot of people. I left after the third bar and went back to the coach house. He had given me his key. "I have another one hidden," he said.

All these fucking secrets, I thought.

When I awakened the next morning Don wasn't there. He hadn't slept in his bed. I went to the office. Sandy was there. We ignored each other. We didn't speak a word. This went on for over a week. I only saw Don before he went out. He had still not slept in his bed. I didn't see my folks that Sunday. I told them I was sick.

Except for one short sentence, "Where are you staying?" and my equally short answer, "Don's place," Sandy and I never talked.

It was an early Saturday afternoon. Don's phone rang. I was alone.

"Hello," I answered.

"It's me," Sandy's voice said. "Can I come over?"

"Sure," I answered.

A short time later, there was a knock at the door. I let Sandy in. I asked how Matthew was. That's all I had to say. She told me he was doing fine. Neither one of us smiled. I showed her around and we had not yet sat down. We stood next to each other in the living room.

"Well, I guess I'll leave," she said.

"Fine," I answered.

I looked at her as we stood close to each other. I felt passion and anger all at once. I couldn't resist. I gripped her shoulders and held them tightly. I looked into her eyes.

I had an erection. I kissed her lips hard. She returned my kiss and I released my grip on her shoulders. She put her arms around me. I pushed her back a little and again looked into her eyes. I was full of animal passion and anger. I just wanted to tear off her clothes and fuck the shit out of her. And that's what I did as she looked into my eyes while we lay naked in bed. I was on top, my movements slow and determined. Our eyes told us we were coming and I was deep and then simultaneously her eyes rolled back and mine did too, while I unloaded a storehouse of frustration that she accepted with her cries. I remained deep in her and gently kissed away her tears as I felt her body tremble.

We lay on our backs and smoked cigarettes. We didn't say a word. After we'd gotten dressed, I walked her out to the courtyard. "I'm sorry I tore your dress," I said.

She smiled.

"Are you going to come home?" she softly asked.

"Sandy, I'm still taking Methedrine. And I don't want to have to sneak."

She looked at me. "You won't have to, but will you promise me you'll boil the needles?"

I gently gripped her shoulders. "Will you boil the needles for me when I ask?"

She paused. "Yes," she answered.

I returned home. I would play with Matthew, we would see my folks. Sandy boiled my needles. Everything was nice. We didn't fight. I had not taken any pictures since the hospital incident. I had tried squinting at distant lights but had not seen anything, so I gave up.

Sandy became pregnant from our encounter at Don's apartment and I was happy for both of us. I stopped taking Methedrine for a while. I gave Melvin a five-hundred dollar retainer to file a lawsuit against Stein. Stein's attorneys answered the suit by denying all allegations made against him. I didn't want the publicity a trial might bring. I was still ashamed. I told Melvin to drop the lawsuit.

One Sunday, I took family pictures with my Rolleiflex, which already had a partly exposed roll of film in it. When I picked up the developed film at the drugstore, I found spirit faces on the pictures that had been taken before the hospital event. I stood in the drugstore, looking at those faces. I had to know. I went over to the pharmacist, who was the manager of the drugstore.

"Excuse me," I asked, "but do you see anything unusual about these pictures I just had developed here?" I handed him two photos.

He looked. "What in the world! What and who are those faces in the window?" he asked in bewilderment.

I smiled.

"Just friends, just friends," I answered. I took my pictures and left. I could feel his stare on my back.

I wondered if I could sell the pictures by mail. I could visualize my ad: *Do Spirit Faces Appear in Photos? Evidence* ... Then I would show just a window, and the words across its glass would read: *In the Window? Send $2.00.* Holy shit. People will be sending me two dollars from all over the whole fucking world, I thought. Wow! I went home and told Sandy to boil my needles. I gave myself a pop in the arm so I could think this through clearly. As I sat on the living room couch, pondering this major coup, I thought about the U.S. Post Office. I'd better get their permission, I decided. The next day at the office, I had Sandy type a letter to the Post Office Department in Washington, D.C., asking for their approval.

Ten days later, I received a reply from the office of the general counsel of the U.S. Post Office. Holy shit, I thought. This must have taken top priority to have an answer back in only ten days, and then from their legal department!

POST OFFICE DEPARTMENT
OFFICE OF THE GENERAL COUNSEL
WASHINGTON, D.C. 20260

Dec. 17, 1964
Mr. Sherwin Ernst
711 West Montrose
Chicago, Illinois 60613

Dear Mr. Ernst:
The receipt is acknowledged of your letter dated December 9, 1964, in which you inquire as to the legality of an enterprise which you propose to conduct through the mails involving the advertisement and sale of "copies

of a picture" which you state you "took in (your) home of a spirit having appeared at a window."

It is impracticable for this office to furnish you an opinion on this matter on the basis of the information furnished by you, since you did not submit a copy of any proposed advertising material with your communication. This office has grave doubts about the authenticity of any such photograph, and if it is represented in advertising matter offering the same for sale that it is a depiction of an actual observed "spirit," I am of the opinion that a post office box should not be rented for use in the operation of the scheme. This Department has in the past issued fraud orders against schemes offering material similar in nature and the Courts have held, in evaluating fraud orders, that where representations made in the sale of such items are so contrary to human experience and common knowledge, proof of falsity of such claims is unnecessary (See Gottlieb v. Schaffer, 141 F. Supp. 7). I am enclosing a copy of the postal fraud statutes for your information.

For the General Counsel:
Sincerely yours,
Julian T. Crornelin
Assistant General Counsel Litigation Division

"I don't believe this."

"What?" Sandy asked.

"This letter from the post office. It's so ambiguous. Just typical lawyer bullshit." I handed Sandy the letter.

"Forget it," I continued, "I'll just have problems. They'll claim it was trick photography."

I put it out of my mind. I had stopped taking Methedrine. Shortly afterward, Sandy miscarried.

We had not renewed our lease on Montrose Avenue. We rented the first floor of a three-story brownstone on Oakdale Street, near Sheridan Road. The living room was long with a high, beamed ceiling. The Oscar Meyer midget had lived there, we were told. It was a few blocks from a park, Lake Michigan, and a boat harbor. I loved that area. I had visited it before, when I had lived in Louisville. It was near a short street that always gave me a feeling of *deja vu* the few times I had walked past its few buildings.

Chapter 11

Several months passed. Late one Saturday evening, we were watching the Irv Kupcinet talk show on television. One of the guests was the Reverend Clifford Royse, Chicago's "Mr. Psychic."

"I'd like to call him and show him the pictures," I said.

Sandy agreed. I wish I had known about him before, I thought. Monday at the office, I gave Sandy her first assignment of the day. "Track down that Clifford Royse," I said. "I want to meet him."

Sandy's really good at following through on orders at the office. Within an hour, she reported back to me.

"He holds psychic classes on Wednesday evenings not far from the office." "Good. We'll go. Get a babysitter," I said.

It was an interesting experience for Sandy and me. We started attending his weekly classes. His specialty was mediumship. He would go into a trance, and spirits would take over his body, their words emanating through his mouth. He found the photos I gave him fascinating. We became friendly; I called him Cliff. One week he told me to bring my camera to the next class; he wanted to do an experiment.

The following week, Sandy and I arrived with my Rolleiflex. Cliff had built a three-sided high cabinet with a black drape on the open side. He hypnotized one of his students who he claimed was very spiritually advanced. He sat him on a chair inside this cabinet while under hypnosis, and pulled down the black drape. Cliff gave me a roll of infrared film. As the student sat with his eyes closed in the darkened cabinet and dimly lit room, in a trance, Cliff would signal for me to snap a picture as soon as he opened the black drape. The idea was to see if I could produce a picture of ectoplasm, which spiritualists consider the manifestation of the existence of a being.

Nothing ever developed showing anything other than the man sitting in a trance inside this cabinet. To me, it was silly and fun. I didn't take it seriously.

Cliff suggested Sandy and I visit Camp Chesterfield, a spiritualist camp in Indiana.

Sandy and I have always been game for new adventures, so we drove the six hours to Camp Chesterfield and spent the night. We attended many group seances for a fee, including a trumpet seance. A person would have to be very gullible to believe what goes on at the camp. However, a camp like that cannot exist on gullible people alone. There must have been actual spiritual experiences by the founder. And I'm sure spiritual events take place today. But to pay a fee for attending a seance and expect something to happen all the time is really being naive. My most memorable recollection of the camp was that coffee was still only a nickel. And we met a man from New York who came to Camp Chesterfield every year to be put in contact with his deceased daughter. It was kind of sad, but maybe not...as long as he was happy. And who knows, maybe he was put in contact. Cliff gave me a letter of endorsement for my pictures in case I wanted to sell them.

March 1965

In regard to the question of psychic or spirit faces, people, or images appearing on photographs, this is a separate study within the vastness of the Extra Sensory Perception field. I have, during my career as a Psychic-Medium, seen thousands of such pictures.

Among the most interesting are the photographs taken by Mr. Sherwin Ernst which appear to show the appearance of hooded figures, as well as other images. I strongly recommend this photograph to be among your collection.

Respectfully,
Rev. Clifford M. Royse Jr.
Director of the Chicago Psychic and Spiritual Center

I got an advertising guy who was moonlighting to draw the ad, which I placed in one of those psychic magazines. I got a response, but then I dropped the ad and lost interest in the pictures, and just concentrated on my insurance business. Sandy was pregnant again, and I had been off Methedrine since leaving Montrose Avenue. The following January, our daughter Lynda was born.

A few years passed; life was very normal. Becky, our housekeeper, was still working for us, my business had grown and Sandy was pregnant again. We hesitantly talked about moving to the suburbs. We weren't sure. We'd go for rides on the weekends, looking at homes. One day we got lost and wound up on a road that dead ended at a forest preserve. There we discovered for sale an English country house with a thatched roof. We both liked the house and the tree-lined street, but we didn't write down the address or the phone number. When we got home, we talked more and more about the quaint home in the quiet neighborhood. We decided we'd like to live there. We drove back the following week. We couldn't find it. We had found it by accident and now it had just vanished. We tried week after week, but it was just not meant to be.

We put off the thought of moving. Later, our son Jon was born and we remained on Oakdale Street for the next year and a half. One Saturday afternoon, while returning alone from the park, I walked down the street where I had always had that sense of *deja vu*. One of the buildings had a sign in front: Condominiums for Sale. I returned home and called the owner. He described the apartment with the view of Lake Michigan and I told him I'd buy it. I told Sandy, who got excited. We saw it the following day and both fell in love with it. The apartment building had just gone condominium.

"We won't have to do a thing to it," Sandy said.

We moved in and lived there through a year of major construction as Sandy found new things to do, starting with the kitchen. I designed my study and I bought our mirrored bedroom set; the rest I didn't care about. My business, now occupying a large space on the top floor of the same building on LaSalle Street, had grown to where I had thirty-five employees and an IBM computer. I was no longer going out selling. I was an executive, dealing with all the problems and pressures that go with that position. The search and need for increased bank lines of credit were constant due to the company's growth, and Sandy would always have my martini ready after receiving my car radio call when I was five minutes from home. We had several different circles of friends, from the rich to the not rich, and we led the good life. We had Becky working for us five days a week and a summer mother's helper who never went home. Sandy and I would often take three-day trips to Paradise Island in the Bahamas. The whole family skied Aspen in the spring, and we returned there for the summer. The two of us went separately to the Esalen Institute in California's Big Sur many times for their five-day Gestalt workshops.

My sister Sylvia visited us several times; I took her to my parents' home and she saw them several times, too. We remained close. My nephew Barry was twenty-one when he first visited and stayed with us. He was good-looking and quick-witted, more like a younger brother to me than a nephew. All of us went to his college graduation, where I saw Sarah for the second time and met her husband, Johnny. We understood why everyone liked him. Seeing Sarah was wonderful, but the big emotion of the first time wasn't there. We just enjoyed each other's presence. My thrill happened at the Beverly Hills Hotel. Sylvia, who was a member of the Hollywood Women's Press Club and Hollywood editor of *Movie Life* magazine, had taken Sandy and me there for a *Photoplay Magazine* award affair. I met John Wayne, and after talking with him, I asked that he stay for a minute; I wanted Sandy to meet him. I've always enjoyed his movies and Sandy never could understand how I could watch him.

"Sandy...follow me. There's someone I want you to meet."

She looked way, way up from her height of five foot one when I introduced her to this six-foot-four giant.

"Hi, Mr. Wayne," she said, "it's nice meeting you."

Back in Chicago, our different circles of friends would have parties. Marijuana was smoked at some of the gatherings, and we always enjoyed joining the crowd. One friend was a booth announcer for CBS. His voice would always come alive delivering the news and doing the voiceover for the slide that the station showed each night as it was about to go off the air. Sandy and I could always tell when Bob was stoned. He would deliver the news like a Shakespearean actor. We'd laugh. He would come to our condominium late, bringing hashish. He and I would smoke hash in a small pipe and play chess.

Sandy would go to bed while we finished our game. Only one of our friends did coke. She brought some over a couple of times for Sandy and me to try. We'd lined the mirrored nightstand in our bedroom and snorted the white powder. It felt good. We got a high but it wasn't our type of drug. We considered it dangerous and expensively addictive and never wanted to pursue it.

Methedrine was taken off the market by its manufacturer in the late sixties. There was a drug in the underground called methedrine, which became popularly known as speed, but it wasn't the same and I never wanted to try it, as I considered the habit dangerous. I would have liked to have the experience of taking LSD under a Timothy Leary-controlled environment or as Aldous Huxley did, watching little green men march in front of him after tripping on mescaline, but those opportunities never presented themselves and I wouldn't consider street stuff.

Our lives were a Jekyll and Hyde situation, and every Sunday afternoon, we would pick up my mother and go over to my cousin Shirley's home in Skokie. Onnie, my father, and Ojeh, in that order, had already died, but the remaining Wicker Park family would all be there. I enjoyed myself there, but since my mind would always wander thinking about the business pressures and money pressures lying ahead the following week, I would enjoy smoking the pipe and playing chess so I could concentrate on something else. Besides, it was always great with sex. The following day, I always had a clear head.

That little itty bitty spark ignited years ago in Wicker Park that had made Deanie, Shirley and me one all for one and one for all had gone. Now they were just my cousins.

And Sandy. Well, I had broken her trust with my affair with Audrey. And she had broken my trust with that hospital fiasco. Why, why, why? Why didn't anyone sit down and talk to me before that ambulance was called? Like the spoons, I thought, I would never know.

My encounters with other women through the years were just part of my life. No regrets, no guilt. My occasional flings were always matinees or when I was out of town. I never took time away from Sandy or the kids. I was always a devoted husband and father. I never wined or dined these women. If we felt mutual attraction, I would just have the woman meet me in front of the LaSalle Hotel, where I'd pick her up in my car and drive to a small classy motel-hotel nearby, where I had an arrangement and a master key. I would just call ahead and have my room number given to me. When I parked the car and we rode up in the elevator no one would even question us. We would just enter the room. None of the women ever refused.

I loved giving head and having head given to me, and they and I also loved to fuck. They would get on top and lose all their inhibitions. Our friendships were strictly sexual, no strings attached. Now I had my secrets too.

One day I got a call in the office from my sister Sylvia. Abe had died. She was hurt when I told her I would not be attending the funeral. But she understood. I had no feelings about his death. It was just a fact. and I went about my life.

The months went by and Sandy and the kids went to Glenwood Springs, Colorado, with her parents. From there, she was to go to Aspen to look at a house we wanted to buy. I stayed home to attend to business. The office was very busy and I had important meetings coming up. Besides, a woman I had met at Esalen and had a relationship with was to be in Chicago that Friday night. She was from Beverly Hills and was beautiful with long red hair and a perfect body. At Esalen she would skip her workshops and I would skip mine. We would lie naked in each other's arms on the grass, atop a secluded cliff and look out over the Pacific. She told me her life story and I listened attentively. I told her my life story- all except the hospital, as she listened attentively. We really liked each other.

I had not done any type of drugs for quite a while. I had two bottles of champagne at home. The beautiful woman was to be there later that evening, and this time, if Sandy called, I would be home.

I was at my health club, where I had played handball, taken a swim and was sitting in my cabana smoking a cigarette. It was already after five and I was looking forward to the evening, when my name was called over the intercom. I picked up the phone. It was my office manager.

"Sherwin," her frantic voice said, "you'd better come to the office right away. I think Marshall had a heart attack, and may be dead. We called an ambulance."

I hung up the phone. "Fuck, shit, cocksucker," I muttered aloud. "Marshall...of all the fucking times to have a heart attack and die."

As I drove to the office, I was still cursing Marshall. Marshall can't be dead, I thought. He's always been a hypochondriac, but this was the extreme.

As I entered the office, my office manager came over to me. She had tears in her eyes.

"He's dead," she sobbed, putting her head on my chest. "The ambulance came and took him away."

Marshall had died of a cerebral hemorrhage. He had taken an aspirin as he always did when he had a headache. He had just finished dictating a letter to his new secretary. He grasped his head and fell face forward onto the desk. He was dead. His wife, Barbara, had called afterward, asking for him. She was told he was in conference.

None of the employees still at work knew what to do. The new secretary typed the letter he had dictated, and left it on my desk for signature. She was unemotional.

"You typed this letter after Marshall died?" I asked. "Yes," she answered.

I called my office manager into my private office.

"That new girl-I like her. She's real good. Don't let her quit."

"Who's going to tell Barbara?" my office manager asked.

"I will. But I don't want to do it by phone. I'll drive out there and break the news...If she calls again, tell her Marshall is still not available."

I announced to my office manager that I wanted all managers and their assistants in the office at nine a.m. sharp. "I

183

don't care if it is Saturday, and some have the day off, they're to be there at nine a.m. or find another job."

With those words, I left and started the long drive on the crowded expressway to Des Plaines- the same suburb where Forest Hospital was located.

As I drove, my thoughts were of Marshall and Barbara. I had known Marshall since I was a kid. He was one year older than I. When I would visit my Wicker Park family, after they had moved to Lyndale Street, I would play with Marshall. He was one of the kids on the block. I knew his mother and father very well. They'll really be sad, I thought. He was an only child. He was drafted into the army and served in Korea during the war. He would write to me and say, "I always knew you would end up in Paris." I had started my business thirteen years ago on forty dollars. At that time Marshall was a comptroller for a die-casting company. He set up my books in his home. Late at night he would order policies from his kitchen table, while Barbara and I would talk.

"'One day, Marshall," I would say, "you'll quit your job, and come to work for me full-time."

Marshall and Barbara were truly soul mates. I could never picture either of them with anyone else. They had a daughter, Cindy and, years later, when they found they couldn't have any more children, they adopted a pretty little blonde girl with big brown eyes. They named her Randi. Sandy and I and the kids had been to their home in Des Plaines several times for dinner. Both Marshall and Barbara had a weight problem, one that wasn't helped by the fact that Barbara was a terrific cook. I loved her endless piles of hamburgers; eating there was an event. Later, Marshall went on a diet and really lost the weight. He looked great.

Many times, before his dieting days, Marshall had gotten on my nerves. I hated the times a message would be put on my desk: Barbara called, Marshall won't be in. He's sick. I could always tell when Marshall was really sick. Those times, he would call me personally. I kept a secret diary on Marshall. It had all the dates and times of calls that he was sick. I had planned to confront him with it one day and compare his days off with the national average. He was an accountant; that he would understand. And the other time he pissed me off was the time he took a part in a musical play. He would rehearse every night and then he would go home and study his lines. "Fuck, he could be working late at the office," I'd mutter.

It was still light out as I parked my car in their driveway. I rang the bell. Their housekeeper answered. "Barbara and the girls went grocery shopping. They should be home soon," she said.

I explained what had happened and she let me in. After a while, I became impatient. I went back outside and leaned against my car. Soon Barbara pulled up and parked in front. I saw her two daughters and all the grocery bags. Barbara got out of the car; so did her daughters.

"Sherwin," she smiled, "what are you doing here?"

As she walked around the car, she looked at me, intuitively knowing that this wasn't a social visit. Her voice quavered. "Sherwin...Marshall, Marshall. Did something happen to Marshall?" she asked frantically.

"Barbara...he died, Barbara!" I put my arms around her and held her tightly, cheek to cheek.

Cindy came to my side, and I held her too. The housekeeper came and took little Randi inside. I couldn't hold back any longer. Suddenly, tears filled my eyes. Barbara and Cindy cried as I forcefully held back my tears and concentrated on consoling them. We went into the house and sat on the living room couch. I sat in the middle with my arms around Barbara and Cindy, comforting them as they cried, kissing their tears.

When I regained my composure, I told Barbara what had happened. We sat like this for a long time. Randi looked at us from across the room. She was too young to grasp what had happened, I thought. And then Barbara and Cindy called Randi over, and they hugged and kissed and cried.

I asked Barbara who we could call. She asked the housekeeper to get a neighbor friend. I just sat with my arms around them, trying to comfort them in their grief. I couldn't wait until help arrived and rescued me from this position. I was now totally composed. Soon help would arrive and then I could leave...I had a date.

The neighbor and her husband came over. They comforted Barbara and the girls.

They made phone calls, and soon family members and friends began to arrive. I couldn't leave. It wouldn't be right. Marshall's mother and father came in. They cried in my arms as I held them.

I arrived home very late that night and called Sandy at the lodge in Glenwood Springs. She was very sad over Marshall's death. She asked me to fly out so just the two of us could spend time in Aspen. I told her that I didn't see how I could get away.

The next morning, I was at the office early, planning the reorganization. As general manager, Marshall had worn many hats. I wanted responsibility delegated fast, and the office ready to go Monday morning with business as usual. Everyone arrived early or on time and, with great esprit de corps, together we accomplished a difficult task. Promotions were given, furniture was moved and someone else now occupied Marshall's office.

After a long day, I drove back to Des Plaines to be with Barbara and her family. The house was full of people and after saying my hellos, I got lost in the crowd. The funeral was set for Monday. Barbara's parents, brother, sister-in-law and uncle were flying in from Seattle. Sunday I went early to the office and finished up some paperwork. I drove to Des Plaines that afternoon. Monday I was in the office very early. The office was busy as usual; it was as if Marshall had never worked there.

I wouldn't let anyone take time off from work to go to the funeral except for Marshall's administrative assistant. She had known Marshall and Barbara for many years and was socially close with them. We drove together to the funeral home. There were at least two hundred people there. As I stood in line to offer my condolences again to the family, Barbara asked me if I would be a pallbearer.

"Sure," I said.

I walked to the rear and looked at the crowd. I started to feel weak and nervous. I walked outside and had a cigarette. I walked back inside the lobby and started to enter the chapel again. The services were about to start. I broke into a cold sweat. I started to panic. I couldn't go through with it. I could not enter that chapel again. If I was a pallbearer, I would drop the casket, I knew. I turned and hurriedly walked to my car and drove away. I parked several blocks away and crawled into the back seat. I was shaking as I closed my eyes and tried to take a nap. After a while, I drove home and called Sandy.

"You'll never believe what I did," I said.

I explained what had happened. I was not emotional or tearful over the experience.

I just could not explain my reaction. It just was not like me.

That evening, I returned to Barbara's home. Everyone was there as I quietly slipped in, embarrassed and expecting them all to stare. No one did. I went over to Barbara. "I'm terribly sorry," I said.

"I understand," she said as she held my hand and kissed my cheek. Never did anyone ever say a word about my leaving the funeral home.

Tuesday, I put in a full day at the office. My desk was back to normal. Wednesday morning I was anxious. I wanted to get away. I wanted to see Sandy and the kids. I called Continental

187

Airlines from the office and booked a first-class seat on an early afternoon flight. I left a message at Sandy's lodge: I'll be there later. I'll call.

I delegated last-minute instructions, drove home, packed and changed into my Colorado clothes and my cowboy boots. I called a cab to take me to O'Hare.

Continental flew nonstop to Denver; from there I would have to rent a car and make the long drive to Glenwood Springs; or I could take a flight from Denver to Aspen, rent a car and drive forty-five minutes back to Glenwood Springs; or, I thought, I could rent a plane in Denver and have them fly me to Glenwood Springs' private airport. I decided on the latter. I asked the ticket counter attendant if she could call ahead and make the arrangements. I wanted a single-engine plane. I said it was an emergency.

"Yes, sir, I'll see what I can do," she said.

When the plane was airborne, an attractive flight attendant came over to my seat.

She leaned forward and spoke softly, "The pilot is working on getting you a private plane."

My adrenaline was going. I was excited, expectant...I thought I could be setting a new world's record in getting from Chicago to Glenwood Springs. It was like my empty desk. I just delegated, and the wheels were put in motion. I leaned the seat back a little as I sipped the first of my two Bloody Marys.

"The passenger who ordered a private plane," the pilot's voice announced, "the pilot will meet you at the gate as you depart."

The stewardess approached. "Your private plane will be ready," she smiled.

"Thank you," I answered.

We landed twenty minutes later. As I disembarked, I had no trouble recognizing the pilot as he repeated my name. No uniform ...he wore sport clothes and held a clipboard. He

188

pointed to the single-engine Cessna within sight of the Continental plane that had just landed. We walked to a nearby flight of stairs that led outside; he carried my small suitcase and called me sir.

When we became airborne, I asked if I could fly. I told him I'd flown over one hundred and fifty hours when I was a young man. He gave me the altimeter height and compass heading and I was in control. As I flew over the snow-topped mountains on this clear day, I was totally relaxed and at peace, in sharp contrast to the frantic pace of late. As we approached Glenwood Springs, I made one steep bank and gave him back the controls.

After I'd called Sandy to pick me up, the pilot and I had a cup of coffee and smoked together in the small airport lounge. Later, I waited outside. He had taxied to the end of the runway for takeoff. Sandy arrived by van from the lodge and we shared a long hug. We watched and waved as the plane left the ground and dipped its wings back and forth as a gesture of farewell.

I had always loved Glenwood Springs, with its long swimming pool fed by sulfur springs. Nearby was a place called Vapor Caves. I would walk there to sweat in the natural steam and then have a massage.

The following day, the kids and my in-laws returned to Denver, and Sandy and I rented a car and drove to Aspen to spend two days. I was short-tempered with Sandy a few times in Aspen. I didn't know why. Maybe it was guilt, I thought. We didn't buy the house in Aspen; I was already stretched too far financially. I didn't need the additional pressure.

I was back in my office early Monday morning and my desk was loaded. I had my desk cleaned by ten and went to the health club. I was the only member there. I played racquetball by myself. I always had an imaginary partner when I played alone. I'd always won before, but today I lost.

I returned to the office. I just didn't have the pep and energy that was always me. I went home late in the afternoon. I closed the door in my study and took a nap on the couch. I didn't want to go anywhere. I just wanted to be alone.

This went on for over a week; it was as if all my energy was being sucked from my body. I had always worked hard and played hard. Now I felt like doing neither. I had an important lunch date with the president and executive vice president of an insurance company. I felt very nervous and uptight talking with them. I knew them both very well; we had done business together for years. But now I just wanted to leave and go home. I went to the washroom and threw cold water on my face. When I came back, I told them I had called the office and that I had an emergency and would have to leave. I drove home and lay on my couch in the study. Sandy was concerned. I explained how I felt that if I didn't leave that luncheon meeting, I was just going to crack up. My hands had been shaking when I went in the washroom. I was at a total loss as to what was happening to me. Am I on the verge of a nervous breakdown, I wondered. I just didn't know. I went in the bathroom and closed the door.

I looked in the mirror. *What is happening to me? What is happening to me?* I watched the tears flow down my face. "I don't believe this," I sobbed.

Sandy knew better than to ever bring up the word *psychiatrist* to me again. I came out of the bathroom. "Sandy, find me a psychiatrist, " I said. She looked at me and I jokingly added, "Don't call Stein."

Sandy found someone who was supposed to be very good. His name was Dr.Bernard Schulman. His office was near our home.

I had an appointment the following day. I explained all I could about how I felt. I told him about my whole life. I didn't leave out anything except how I liked to give head. But all he'd have had to do was ask and I would have told him that too.

I made light of what was happening to me; telling it humorously made me feel better. His assistant gave me an inkblot test. "What do you see?" she asked.

"An inkblot," I answered.

She laughed. "Really, what do you see?"

"Really, I only see an inkblot. What am I supposed to see?"

I knew she wouldn't have seen things from my pictures years ago, so why should I see things in her inkblots, I thought. I refused to give in.

I saw Dr. Schulman early the next afternoon. I told him how I had cried the night before, alone in the bathroom, for no apparent reason. I explained how I couldn't cope with more than two hours at most in the office. "I went home," I said.

He wanted me to check into the hospital. "You have battle fatigue," he stated. "I want to run tests."

"What hospital?" I asked.

"St. Joseph," he said.

"Where in St. Joseph?"

"The psychiatric ward."

"No way ...I'll never go to a psychiatric ward again. Can you check me into the regular hospital?"

He hesitated. "All right, I'll get you admitted as a regular patient."

"What are you going to have done to me?"

"I want you to get rest. You'll be given massive doses of Librium."

"Bunches of pills?" I asked.

"No...injectably."

"Injectable librium. Massive doses," I exclaimed.

"Yes."

I used every ounce of strength I had left in my body to hold back the smile that wanted to spread across my face.

"All right, if you really think that's what I need," I answered seriously.

Dr. Shulman's assistant made arrangements for me to check into the hospital. I had time to go home and pack my toilet articles, robe and slippers. A young married couple we were friendly with was there. They knew I hadn't been feeling good lately. I announced to Sandy and our friends, David and Phylis, that I had battle fatigue and was going to check into the hospital for rest and tests. David and Phylis were with the Goodman Theater and said they would stop by to see me later in the hospital. I had been interviewed several times on radio and television, and the host and I had talked about insurance, on which I was considered an expert of sorts. David and Phylis had helped me with diction on a few words I've mispronounced all my life as a result of spending my youth in the Haymarket district of Louisville. One of those words was we'll. I have always pronounced it as *wheel*: "Call my office, *wheel* help you find the right policy."' To me, that sounds natural. "We will" sounds phony. And "we'll" turns out...*wheel*.

To my ear it sounds right.

They left. Sandy was upset that they would be visiting me in the hospital if I was supposed to be getting rest.

"Don't worry, they won't stay long. And I've always enjoyed their company."

I packed my few things and walked to the nearby St. Joseph Hospital. My thoughts were on my slipped disk surgery, a few years earlier. I'd had back problems for years, and three years before, my back went out at our new condominium. I had trouble getting up off the toilet seat but managed to make it down to the bathroom floor; from there I couldn't move without excruciating pain. That time I had Sandy call the doctor and an ambulance to take me to the hospital. I had a herniated disk. They performed a laminectomy. It was major surgery, and when they threw me back onto my bed, the doctor told me they would be giving me morphine for pain.

"Can I have anything else?" I asked.

"Demerol," he answered.

"Anything else?"

"Codeine."

"How often?"

"Every four hours, until the pain goes away."

"OK. Thanks, doctor."

They gave me a shot of morphine. Four hours later, I asked for Demerol, and later, codeine. Hell, I wasn't even in pain, but I never told them that. I'd always look at my watch, and if the nurse was five minutes late, I buzzed. I would give my choice of drug. Sandy couldn't believe it. Finally, days later, I was looking at one of the plants a friend had sent. As I stared at it with one tired eye open, I noticed that it was beginning to look like a rooster. At that point, I told the nurse, "My pain's gone. I don't need any more drugs."

Hospital orthopedic wards are really loose with drugs. Most people are in real pain.

I never had any.

I was looking forward to the massive doses of injectable Librium as I checked into the hospital for my battle fatigue rest.

After I settled into my private room and put on the short hospital gown, the nurse came in and gave me the first shot in the ass.

"How often will I be getting this?" I asked.

"Every four hours. If you have to go to the washroom, buzz and I'll help you walk."

Thirty minutes later, I had to go. I didn't buzz; I didn't think I'd have any trouble. I wobbled as I walked.

"Wow! This stuff is good, and I've only had my first," I murmured.

I returned to my bed and looked at my watch. "Wow! I don't believe this shit," I chuckled.

I called Sandy. "Hi," I said.

I told her what I was taking. She saw no humor in it. I hung up. Later, after my second shot, David and Phylis arrived. I told them to give me a diction lesson. We were all laughing. The phone rang. It was Sandy.

"What's all the laughing about?" she asked.

I explained. "Wheel be here if you want to come over," I slurred, laughing. Sandy didn't see any humor in it. She hung up.

Early the next morning, I was surrounded by doctors with white jackets. St. Joseph was a teaching hospital and I was really interrogated. I told them I had battle fatigue. I was informed that Dr. Shulman would be seeing me later that morning.

When Dr. Shulman arrived he asked the usual question: "How are you?"

I told him that getting this type of rest was just what I needed. I hadn't cried, I hadn't thought about the office. He's a miracle worker, I thought.

I called Sandy again. She couldn't stand my enjoyment. I hung up. I called David and Phylis and I enjoyed our conversation. This went on for six days. It was a Friday evening and they were late for my 11 o'clock shot. I was very patient; I waited until 11:10 and then I buzzed.

"Yes, may I help you?" the late shift nurse asked.

"My shot-you forgot it."

"Dr. Shulman said you are not to receive any more shots. Here, I have a sleeping pill for you."

"I don't want a sleeping pill. I want my shot."

"Sorry, you can't have any more."

My voice rose slightly. I told the nurse that there must be some mistake. "Dr. Shulman never mentioned taking me off the Librium."

The nurse said she had written orders. I demanded to see someone in charge. The charge nurse entered my room. She confirmed that I was not to be given any more Librium.

"You call Dr. Shulman and tell him I want to speak to him."

They wouldn't do it. I called Sandy. I was angry. "Call Shulman. Tell him I want one last shot"

Sandy sided with Shulman. I hung up. I called David and Phylis and told them what had happened. They were sympathetic.

"Listen," I said, "if I don't get one last shot, I'm checking out. Can I stay with you?"

"Sure," David said.

I buzzed the nurse.

"If I don't get one last shot, I'm checking out." She sent the on-call doctor into my room.

"You don't cut someone off without advance notice. Unless I get one more shot, I'm leaving."

He said no and walked out.

I called David and Phylis. "I'm coming over, Phylis. Can I sleep on your couch?"

"Sure," she said.

I staggered to the closet and put on my clothes.

I gathered all my belongings and I was ready to go. Three nurses and two doctors entered the room

"You can't leave," they said.

"Try and stop me," I answered. "This ain't no psycho ward."

They all looked at me in astonishment. One of the doctors said I would have to sign a release paper if I left.

"Fine, " I said.

I signed the release form and with all the strength and determination I could gather, I walked a straight line to the elevator. I grabbed a cab outside and gave the driver David and Phylis' address.

The three of us sat in the living room and talked. I was exhausted and very sleepy. I laid my head down and fell asleep. I slept for almost twenty-four hours. When I woke up, Phylis told me she had called Sandy to let her know that I was there.

"I'm going home," I said.

When I arrived home, Sandy was not angry. She seemed concerned.

"I called Phylis just after you left. David said you lurched down the hallway to the elevator and went home."

"Yep. I'm going to sleep again." I got undressed and went to bed; that bed really felt good.

Early the next morning, I was at my office. I put in a full day and went home.

Later that evening I cried for no apparent reason. I just cried. I felt weak and helpless. I didn't know what to do. The next morning, I called Dr. Shulman and saw him that afternoon at his office.

He felt I had a chemical imbalance and wanted to prescribe medication. Lithium. "What's that for?" I asked.

"Manic depression."

"Manic depression!" I exclaimed.

"Yes."

"Does it come injectably?"

"No. You would be taking a pill." I was disappointed.

"Do you think I'm manic depressive?"

"Yes. You have a chemical imbalance."

"How long will I have to take the pill?" "Probably forever."

"Forever!" I exclaimed.

"Yes."

"Dr. Shulman, I just find it hard to believe that I'm manic depressive." I paused,

"All right...I'll try it."

I was seeing Dr. Shulman once a week. Three weeks had already passed since I had started taking lithium. I was still crying every night alone, locked up in my bathroom or the study. I started to analyze myself ...going as far back as I could remember. I tried to recall all the events of my entire life. I recalled Wicker Park...I remembered the hospital room when I had my tonsils removed ...I remembered another little boy in the room, telling me I'd get ice cream after my tonsils were out. I could picture everything about the apartment and my family. My thoughts shifted to Louisville ...when I had played high school football and quit. I felt so guilty. I had let everyone down. And Coach Dennis...he was so disappointed. Everyone loved Coach Dennis.

Every evening I would reflect as I recalled events of the past, and I'd bring forth feelings of guilt. I'd think of my mother and then Sarah and feel guilty. I thought about when I was a kid and I'd told my mother to go fuck herself. And then I would cry and go in the bathroom and lock the door; I'd shower and sit naked on the floor in the locked bathroom. I would place my Zippo lighter on the floor and a cigarette across its top as a symbol of a cross. I would cross my legs on the floor and move them close to my body as I sat with my back straight, staring at the cross, and then close my eyes. This is weird, I thought, but I did it every morning and every evening. It was the only time the feelings of helplessness and sadness would be gone. It was a ritual, a very strange ritual. But I felt at peace whenever I performed this act. Later, I would recall so many things that would bring up guilt, and the tears would flow.

Sandy felt helpless. She was very compassionate. One evening we were invited by friends to dinner and a play. I begged off but told Sandy to go. They picked her up at our home.

"I'm not feeling well," I explained.

197

The three of them left and I stayed alone in my closed study, sitting on my leather couch reflecting, with tears flowing.

As I sat, in the depths of my mind I had a flash: *My God, why didn't I think of this before?* My gosh...yes, yes, I thought. The *Zadik*. The *Zadik*. If anyone can help me, it would be the *Zadik*. He had saved me before. Before, when I saw those two huge eyes staring at me, he saved me, and then he healed me. I turned to look at the window, the window in the study, the window out of which I would always watch the sun rise over Lake Michigan on a clear early, early morning. Yes, yes...the *Zadik* could help me.

I stood up and went to the window. I spoke aloud softly, the tears flowing. *Zadik*, I cried. *Zadik...please help me, please help me*, I prayed. *Please show yourself to me but not in human form. I don't want you here...I don't want those spirits back. I have a family ...I don't want that again. Please, can't you help me...without appearing.*

I sat back on the couch. I turned my head to the left to look at the window. I could distinguish the spirit outline of the *Zadik* forming. Please don't enter, I begged. Please help me...but don't enter, I pleaded. Then I picked up the pen in front of me and started to write. My body felt different. It felt receptive, and the words I wrote felt guided. I wrote very, very fast. And when I was through, I slowly read the words I had written:

The way to eliminate feelings of guilt is to learn the art of disassociation. Association and dissociation under separate sources of consciousness can separate favorable and unfavorable thoughts, thus memory links would consist of favorable interactions and favorable actions plus unfavorable actions. Example: mathematically there would never be a minus in a grouping of plusses, thus semantically, guilt feelings would not exist.

I felt total understanding as I read what I had just written. It all made sense to me. I had been creating feelings of guilt on an unconscious level, and releasing those feelings of energized guilt through tears. That negative energy created a chemical imbalance that weakened my very being. I now had insight into the problem. He showed me thought forms in the shape of rings-memory links. I now had the ability to control my thoughts and place them in their proper space. If I was to think of my mother, she would have her own space, which would be connected only to favorable memories of past events. Sarah would have her own space, away from my mother. The thoughts of my affairs with different women would be removed from the space Sandy was in. Sandy's space would consist of our good times. Our children could be put in that space. Any bad times would have their own unconnected link, far removed in space.

I understood totally. I walked to the clear window and sat down with my crossed legs brought close to my body as some yogis do. I placed my Zippo lighter on the floor, a cigarette across its width. I looked at the cross I had formed. I closed my eyes and sat erect. With my thumbs, I massaged my facial bones. I pressed my temples, points below my chin, the back of my neck. My thumbs pressed on the nerves.

"Thank you, *Zadik*," I whispered.

I stood up...I was energized. I felt like my old self. I knew I would not cry again.

I knew my strength had returned.

Sandy came home. She saw the joy in my face. "Are you all right?" she asked.

"Sandy, I'm fine...I'm OK now."

"Are you sure you're all right?" she asked cautiously.

"Yes...you go to sleep. I'll talk to you tomorrow."

Sandy went to sleep. I went into the bathroom and locked the door. I sat in that strange position and placed the Zippo lighter and cigarette in front of me. I pressed on my nerves with both thumbs. It was automatic. It was natural. I felt that my thumbs were being guided to press the nerves of my temples, cheekbones, front and back of the neck. I performed these exercises for thirty minutes. I went to bed. It was the earliest I had retired in months. I felt at peace.

Sandy's side of the bed was closest to the window overlooking Lake Michigan. She was sound asleep. I lay on my side at the far edge of our king-size bed with my back to Sandy. I wasn't sleepy-just peaceful. My eyes were open in the darkened room dimly lit by the stars and the moon. I gazed at the closet door six feet away. A shadow appeared ...the shadow of the *Zadik*. I quietly whispered, "*Zadik*, thank you so much, but please do not materialize in my home." I closed my eyes. I felt a tingle throughout my body. I saw a white mist from the back of my head. And suddenly, the mist opened and I was pulled far, far away...way up high. I saw a planet to my left. And out of nowhere, to the right of the planet, in some distant space, appeared a man, wearing a very large turban and a colorful robe that covered him up to his neck. His face was angelic with its smile.

Is this a dream, I wondered. I opened my eyes...and saw the shadow of the *Zadik*. I closed my eyes and the man, this swami, was still there. The sensation throughout my body was one of ecstasy. This isn't a swami, I thought. The large orange turban, his beardless face- I saw him from the rib cage up. This was a guru. He had just appeared out of nowhere. Out of the East. This was my guru. The *Zadik* had led me to my guru.

I could now feel the angelic peaceful smile on my own face. But nothing could compare to the angelic smile on this guru. Then suddenly, I heard a voice-not an outer voice, but the voice of my soul. I heard it within the chamber of my ear; the guru was talking to me-telepathically, not with his words, but with his thoughts. And my soul spoke aloud within me, and those thoughts became words I could hear. The guru drew me closer to him and I looked to his right side and down below. I saw the planet Earth and I saw the past, present and future all at once. I looked at the guru and I spoke to him. My thoughts were spoken by my soul. I asked questions. The guru gave me answers.

His lips did not move, but his thoughts were spoken by my soul and I heard his answers. I opened my eyes a little just to make sure this was no dream. The shadow of the *Zadik* on the closet door was still there. I closed my eyes and the guru was still there, way up on high. The total ecstasy was indescribable. It was complete bliss. We held a conversation. My soul spoke his words. The guru materialized the mass of thought and then showed me what and how what I had written earlier exists, how it functions, how I could always control the links of memories. This total bliss lasted for what seemed an eternity.

The guru told me that I was a guru. "How am I a guru?" I asked.

"You are a guru to your family."

"May I stay with you?"

"If you wish," the guru answered.

I thought...not now. I want to be a guru to my family, but...

"May I see you again?" I asked.

"Yes, all you have to do is knock and I will be there."

With those words of the guru, spoken aloud within the chamber of my ears by my soul, I then felt a quiet forceful release of gas. And then all was gone. The guru was gone. I opened my eyes. The shadow of the *Zadik* was fading.

"Thank you, *Zadik*," I said as I closed my eyes and fell into a peaceful sleep.

I awakened fully energized and at peace. I showered and put my razor to my face.

I stared at my face in the mirror. I did not want to shave. I felt naked not having a beard. I knew that if I wanted, I could be like the *Zadik*. I could knock all the time and be with my guru. I forced myself to shave. I was dressed when Sandy got out of bed. Through the open bathroom door she saw me emptying the bottle of Lithium pills into the toilet.

"What are you doing?" she asked.

"I don't need these any more," I answered as I flushed the pills down nine stories.

As I drove to the office I felt totally detached from the world around me. The traffic, the pedestrians were all just a passing parade and incidental. I was above the crowd. I was an observer. My work at the office was effortless. I canceled all future appointments with Schulman. I was in a state of ecstasy and detachment. My crying days were over. I was totally cured of any problems. I had no interest in women, drugs or adventure. I wanted to be a guru to my family-that was all that mattered.

That evening, alone with Sandy in the study, I told her of my experience. She became lost in my words and became part of the experience. She was at peace along with me as I explained, "The *Zadik* appeared in a shadow or spirit form on the window in the study. I pleaded for him to help. I felt so helpless; he was the only one who could help me, I knew. I wrote these words very fast, as if my writing were being guided."

I showed Sandy my scribbles. She could read my scrawl but I read the words aloud to her.

"Do you understand?" I asked. "Well, not exactly," she said.

I explained the many cells that everyone possesses-how these cells are linked to other memory cells.

"Let me give you an example," I said. "When my sister, Sylvia, called six months ago about Abe-when he died-well, I didn't want to go to the funeral. Sylvia was disappointed. I felt guilty about not being with her. I should have gone for her. Now I have this memory of Abe and part of that memory is guilt for Sylvia. Do you understand that?"

"Yes."

"Well, when Marshall died, my memory cell of Marshall got linked to the memory of Abe. It didn't belong in that space next to the memory of Abe. But somehow it became transferred there. This memory of Marshall next to the memory of Abe created guilt. When I thought of Marshall, I also unconsciously thought of the guilt of not going to be with Sylvia. That wrongful link of those two memory cells created a chemical imbalance. Marshall's death became all mixed up with Abe. The energy from that mixture forced a chemical secretion across some biologic membranes that created a physiological change in my body. Now can you understand what I'm saying?"

"Yes."

"Now a chain reaction was started. All my memory cells became dislodged and resettled in the wrong space. These memory cells were now linked to memory cells of different thoughts and experiences. I was totally mixed up. It would be like you thinking of me. It would be like you thinking of the kids. Those two memory cells belong linked together. Our family vacations-those memories belong linked with me and the kids. But remember Audrey?"

"Yes, I remember Audrey. " She frowned.

"Well, if that memory cell of Audrey is linked to your memory cell of me, you're going to get pissed all the time. But if that memory cell of Audrey is linked to other unfavorable memories in a different space, it won't piss you off when you think of me. Now do you get it?"

"Hmm."

"See, all you have to do is make sure all your good memory cells are linked together with other favorable cells. You can move them around once you've brought them to a conscious level. Then put all the unfavorable cells in a separate chain. And mathematically never mix minuses with plusses. Do you understand?"

"I think so."

"Practice...If you practice what I just told you, you'll be at peace with yourself. I explained about my sitting position, "like one of those yogis from India. "You mean the lotus position."

"Yeah, that's it," I answered.

I told about my pressing pressure centers on my body, and then I told about my enlightenment with this guru on another plane and what he looked like. I explained how I visually saw with this opening through the back of my head the physical form of my thoughts and memory cells, how I saw the formation of the chain of links made up of memory cells. I explained how this guru had taught me to move them around at will, how I had looked down at planet Earth and seen all of prehistoric time and mankind and history all at once. The past, present and future were motionless and within my sight. It was all now!

"My soul was communicating with the soul of the guru...he imparted all knowledge to me," I explained. "It's very difficult to explain the feeling I had. The closest I can come is when I took Matthew to the park to fly a kite. Remember how I would tell you that when I was a kid in Louisville, I could never get a kite to fly...because it was almost never windy there."

"Yes."

"Well, when I went to the park with Matthew, I didn't expect us to get the kite in the air then, either. And when Matthew and I ran together, pulling the kite with the string, and then the kite became airborne and then Matthew and I stood close together holding the string, and all of a sudden the kite lifted real high and it was totally airborne. There was a moment in time when the realization of that kite being airborne existed. That moment was a thrill for Matthew, but one thousand times more thrilling for me. Now take that feeling I had for a short moment and multiply that time by ten thousand, and then maybe you'll get a glimpse of the feeling I had with that guru."

Sandy was mesmerized by my words. Lightning could have struck our building, but all she would be able to hear would be my words. I had just become a guru to Sandy. Now with my children, I would give them different words of wisdom and I would be like a guru to them too. This is what my guru meant when he told me to be a guru to my family, I thought. I was in a state of complete ecstasy for the next two weeks.

Everything I did at work and at home was totally effortless. I could have lived forever in that state of mind. I was oblivious of all except my immediate family. All others were just passers-by in life's parade. That state of mind continued over the next two weeks and settled into a mood of complacency that would remain for months and in a lot of ways for the rest of my life.

I had told the story of my enlightenment to only a few very close friends. They all became mesmerized when I told my tale. And Sandy did too, each time she heard it again. A close friend was visiting our home with her son and new daughter-in-law from Australia. I told my story and when I was through, the Australian asked if I had ever read the book *Autobiography of a Yogi*.

"No," I said.

"You should," she answered, "you would probably enjoy it."

The following week, I bought the paperback. I was fascinated by the life of Paramahansa Yogananda. His experiences were of an unbelievable nature--even for me. But I had an open mind and became spellbound by his astonishing experiences. I spent several hours each evening reading his book. Then one evening, I turned the page. I couldn't believe my eyes as I looked at a picture of Paramahansa Yogananda with Luther Burbank, the horticulturist.

"My God," I said, "that's him ...that's him."

My body became energized with a surge of feelings of love and discovery.

"Sandy, come here." I spoke softly across the open doors of our bathroom between the study and the bedroom.

"What, hon?" she asked as she entered the study.

"That's him," I said.

She took the book I held out opened to the page with the picture. She looked.

"That's who?"

"The man in the turban. He's my guru."

She studied the picture. She scanned the cover of the book. "But he's dead," she said.

"I know that...but he's alive on another plane." She sat next to me and studied the picture more.

"Are you sure?" she asked.

"Sandy, I could never forget that face, that angelic face. Yes, I'm sure...that's him."

The next day, at the office, I called the Self-Realization Fellowship Lake Shrine in California that had been mentioned in Yogananda's book. It was where Yogananda had led many of his spiritual practices, according to the book. I spoke with a Brother Sarvananda, whom I asked, "Has anyone claimed, in recent years, to have seen Yogananda on the inner plane?"

"Yes...a few people claim to have seen Yogananda on the inner plane in recent years as he looked in his early thirties."

"Thank you very much," I answered as I laid the receiver down. With that thought, I effortlessly finished my day's work and returned home to be with my family.

Several months later a friend who knew the story of my enlightenment called me excitedly, after having read a speech given by Yogananda at a temple in Hollywood, California, on October 8, 1944. He read aloud the following promise that Yogananda had made in the speech, which he had found in a book written by Yogananda, called *Man's Eternal Quest and Other Talks*.

"So long as there is a weeping brother by the wayside, I will come again into this world to wipe away his tears. Why should I be content to enjoy the blessings of heaven while others are suffering?"

Those words touched my soul and after a long silence, I softly said, "He kept his promise."

Chapter 12

Through the following years, our family created memories that will last a lifetime.

Skiing vacations, trips to the Bahamas and Acapulco, a week on a small boat that left San Diego and followed the migration of the gray whales into Baja California. Involvement with school affairs and weekly family jaunts to Chicago's wonderful museums, aquarium and planetarium. I spent all my free time with Sandy and the kids. We always managed to see my mother once a week. We continued to see Uncle Sam, Deanie, Shirley and their families. We had a close circle of friends that we saw frequently. My running around with women had ended, too. The drug use had ceased except on occasion, when my friend Bob would come over late and we would smoke the small pipe and play chess.

The kids would go to three separate out-of-state camps during the summers and Sandy and I would visit during parents' weekends. The two of us would take three-day vacation trips to Paradise Island in the Bahamas.

It was there that I met a swami one morning at the crack of dawn. Sandy slept while I strolled the deserted white sand beach far from the hotel. I approached a dark skinned man sitting in the lotus position, facing the ocean as the sun began to peek above the distant horizon. His eyes opened and he smiled at me.

"Did I interrupt your meditation?" I asked softly.

"No...I was finished and I am going to my houseboat," he replied in a kindly voice with a distinct accent.

I had heard there was a swami who lived on a houseboat nearby and I knew that this was he.

I smiled. "May I go with you? I have some questions to ask."

"Yes. Follow me."

The swami's name was Vishnu Devananda and he had a retreat beyond the beach where we had met. We walked in silence, side by side, past beautiful gardens to his houseboat. We sat on its deck and I told him about the *Zadik* and Yogananda. I told the swami about the jewel the *Zadik* wore on his forehead the first time I saw him sitting in that high-backed wicker chair across my yard.

"That was not a jewel on his forehead. That was his third eye," Vishnu explained.

I felt I was in the presence of a saint. So few words were spoken, but so much was said. I was aglow, just being next to him. He invited me back that evening for dinner and chanting at his retreat.

"Bring your wife," he said.

Sandy returned that evening with me. I introduced her to my new friend and we ate and later chanted with many others during a ceremony on the beautiful candlelit grounds of the retreat. It was a wonderful experience.

Sandy was impressed by his angelic smile. "He's a saint," I said.

When we returned to Chicago, we were invited by friends to their home for a small party. The hosts introduced us to a couple; he was a printer. His name was Sonny. He and I hit it off and I mentioned the story of the swami Sandy and I had just met. Sonny was impressed with my story, and he told me about his guru.

"You have a guru?" I asked. "Yes."

"Where does he live?" "India."

His guru's name was Kirpal Singh and Sonny had been initiated by him in Chicago years ago. I was fascinated by the story of Sonny's guru.

"I'd like to learn more about him," I said.

"Call me Monday and come to my business and I'll give you books to read that he has written."

Early Monday morning I was at Sonny's printing shop. I saw the picture of Kirpal Singh on Sonny's desk. Sonny's guru had a gray beard and wore a white turban. He was retired from a high position in the Indian government. He lived in the foothills of the Himalayas and people from all over the world would come to visit. He would never accept money, and occasionally, he made a world tour.

I asked for his address in India. "I want to write this man," I said.

I left Sonny's shop with his guru's address and three small books: *The Teachings of Kirpal Singh, Volumes I, II and III*.

As I sat in my office, I wrote my letter:

Dear Sant Kirpal Singh Ji Maharaj;

I have a guru who lives on another plane. I have seen him, and he has enlightened me. I love my wife and children, and although I know the ecstasy of enlightenment, and that it is available to me, I have decided to remain with my family - outwardly practicing the customs acceptable by my society. Time and space will pass soon enough, and I shall enter the kingdom of enlightenment, most assuredly, in the destined time.

In the meantime, I would like very, very much to meet you. There are a few answers I seek.

Bless you, Sherwin Ernst

When I finished, I called the post office to get the correct postage and then walked down the corridor and dropped the envelope into the glass mail chute.

After work, I went to my health club to play racquetball and swim. Bob came over late that night and we smoked the pipe and played chess. He left me some hashish as a present, and after he had left, I smoked my pipe in bed and began reading the *Teachings of Kirpal Singh, Volume I,* while Sandy slept. There were words in the book I had never heard before: "The Sat Purush will take him to Alakh, Agam and Anami, stages of imperceptible, inconceivable and nameless God." But then the letters of the written words became alive with energy that I could see, and suddenly I began to comprehend the hidden meaning of every word. *Wow,* I thought, the word and I have become one. I saw and felt, deep within, the knowledge that was written for all to discover. This knowledge was before my eyes. These were words of Godly wisdom that I was understanding.

"How fortunate I am," I thought.

The following nights, I smoked my pipe and read volumes II and III. I told Sandy that there were hidden meanings in every word. The words came alive as my eyes and being experienced their reality. I understood the depth of each word and its true meaning, and I understood the meaning of those strange words. I thought to myself that Alfred Korzybski, the father of semantics, would be my student if he were still alive. "Sandy," I said, "I have to meet this man."

I read aloud passages from the book and Sandy became spellbound as I explained their hidden meaning. Every night, when I finished reading, I would look over at Sandy sleeping. I would gently kiss her shoulder, her neck, her cheek, until she would awaken and embrace me. God...I loved sex.

I called Sonny. "Sonny; I have to meet your guru. Let's go to the Himalayas."

I got Sonny really excited about going to India to see his guru. He had never been there before.

"First, I have to write and get his permission, and then a few months later, we can go," he said.

"Write today, Sonny. Don't put it off."

"OK, Sherwin, but I couldn't go until October."

"OK, set it up for October."

In the month of July, I received a letter from Kirpal Singh:

Dear Sherwin Ernst;

I have received your loving letter of May 28, 1974 and noted its contents.

You state that your Guru has enlightened you and he lives on another plane. It is not clear as to how you could contact him or vice versa i.e. if you happened to leave your body to visit that plane or your Guru came to you in physical body to enlighten you. You may elucidate for further advice.

Howsoever I am pleased to know that you are aspiring for spiritual progress. It is due to the evolution of some rare noble karma of past lives that one yearns for spiritual progress. The gracious Master Power controlling and guiding the destiny of child humanity leads the sincere seekers to the Living Master. There is food for the hungry and water for the thirsty.

You are advised to attend the local Satsang, obtain some printed books relating to the holy Path and study them diligently for grasping theory, which precedes practice. When you feel satisfied and desire to be initiated into the Mysteries of the Beyond, you may apply through the local representative and necessary arrangements will be made for putting you on the way back to God.

There are certain essential basic prerequisites which comprise of total elimination of all meat, fish, fowl, eggs both fertile and unfertile and all alcoholic intoxicants and drugs. If you are already abiding by the same much better, otherwise please try to adapt yourself to this type of serene living in the larger interests of your inner spiritual progress.

With all love and best wishes,
Yours affectionately,
Kirpal Singh

I showed Sonny the letter and a copy of the letter I had sent. Sonny wanted me to go to a local meditation and reading meeting that he called a satsang.

"Thanks, Sonny, but I'm not interested in joining any groups. I've got a guru. His name is Paramahansa Yogananda. He's dead and I went to him on the astral plane, and he told me all I have to do is knock. But as I wrote your guru..." I read aloud part of my letter: "I have decided to remain with my family, outwardly practicing the customs acceptable by my society. Time and space will pass soon enough, and I shall enter the kingdom of enlightenment, most assuredly, in the destined time." I paused. "But I would like to talk to your guru. I just have a burning desire to meet him," I explained.

Sonny called me, months later, just before we were to go to India. His guru had passed away. Sonny was very sad, and I was very disappointed that I would never meet Kirpal Singh.

Bob got into a shouting match with a co-worker at the CBS studio while Walter Cronkite was there, and Bob was fired. He was very despondent and quit coming over to play chess. The years passed and I was totally involved with business and my family.

My mother was now in a nursing home. My business took a downward turn and I felt the pressures. Stocks that used to go up went down. Bank lines of credit tightened.

Volume decreased. Interest rates were high.

A few years later, I sold my business under very unfavorable terms. It was a stupid mistake on my part, and we moved to Boulder, Colorado, where we lived in the mountains. Boulder is a great place. We really enjoyed it there.

I had a small office on the second floor of a building on Boulder's outdoor mall. It was nice and I sat with my feet on the desk and looked at the mountains each day. I was a business broker and I wasn't doing much business myself and my money was slowly running out. One day, I got a call from the chairman of the board of a publicly traded insurance company. I knew him from Chicago and had done business with his company. He offered me a job in Florida as the person in charge of their offices throughout the state.

"How much does it pay?" I asked.

He told me and I said, "I'm really flattered that you offered me this position ...but it's really not enough money. And besides, I love Boulder."

"Fly down. Let's talk; we can work something out," he said.

Sandy was excited about the idea of moving to Florida, so I flew to their Ft. Lauderdale headquarters and met the chairman of the board there. He lived in Chicago and needed someone to take away his headaches. He offered me what I wanted plus a car, a contract plus bonus and a company condominium to stay in until my family moved down.

"And an expense account?" I asked.

"Yes," he answered. "Sherwin, you can live anywhere in the state you want.

There's over one hundred employees and knowing you, you'll just delegate out the work and be on the golf course or beach every day. We don't care as long as you get the job done."

We flew to different parts of the state to see the various offices and I said, "Let me think about it, and I'll let you know."

I returned to Boulder and told Sandy the story. "You said you'll think about it," she exclaimed.

"Yes, I said I'll think about it." "Sherwin, we're running out of money."

"Yeah, I guess you're right I'll take the job."

The plan was that I would take the job and Sandy and the kids would move in six months after selling the house. We couldn't pull Lynda and Jon out of school right away. Lynda was in high school and Jon in junior high. Matthew was not a problem. He was attending the University of Colorado in Boulder and living in a fraternity house. It was sad for all us as we said our good-byes at a hotel in Boulder and I climbed into the hotel van. As the van drove off, my eyes were teary as I looked back and saw them wave.

A six-month separation was wishful thinking. Sandy had trouble selling our home.

I flew back and forth several times. Sandy flew down twice. Matthew came to Ft. Lauderdale on spring break with a fraternity brother. Lynda flew down for a week. Jon never came. He took a sabbatical from school at the age of fifteen and was touring all the western states playing keyboard in a rock band.

We were apart for a year and a half. Our friends couldn't believe Sandy had let me be a bachelor for that period of time in Ft. Lauderdale. I really missed my family! Late one afternoon, after having been in Ft. Lauderdale over four months, on the Fourth of July I went to a place called Yesterday's. I sat at the bar and drank a club soda. There were two women nearby. They smiled at me and I went over to them. There was excitement and sparks between one of them and me on this Fourth of July. We had dinner at Yesterday's... later we danced.

We saw each other frequently for over a year. We became the best of friends. She was beautiful and had long red hair, and when Sandy would call me at the office and say "where were you all night? I called all night." I'd calmly reply, "Out on a boat ...strictly business."

A year later, I woke up one morning with a numbness and tingling sensation in my right leg. That evening I became concerned, even though I felt fine. I went to the emergency room of a nearby hospital.

"You just had a transient ischemic attack," the doctor said.

"What's that?" I asked.

"A mini-stroke. We have to admit you."

"What will you do?"

"Give you Valium to bring your blood pressure down."

"A pill!"

"No. Intravenously and then a shot every four hours."

"Intravenously ...shots!" I said in disgust "All right, if you have to... you have to." Two days later the doctor came to my room in the evening.

"Well, we got your blood pressure down. I'll prescribe medication and you can go home tomorrow morning. And see me at my office next week. By the way, you're going to have to quit smoking."

"Thanks, doctor."

He was leaving my room. "Doctor," I softly called out.

He stopped by the doorway, turning to look at me. "Yes?"

"May I ask you a favor?"

"What, Sherwin?"

"May I have one last shot?"

He smiled. "All right, I'll tell the nurse."

Chapter 13

My uncle Sam had died. So had Deanie. All that was left of the Wicker Park family was my mother, Shirley and I. My mother was still in the nursing home and I flew to Chicago twice and saw her there. She was lonely and sick and wished she were dead.

For both our sakes, I did, too.

I received a call from the nursing home. "Your mother is sick and in the hospital. They don't expect her to survive."

I called the doctor and he confirmed what I had been told. "Call me when she expires," I said.

I flew to Chicago for the funeral. I stayed with Shirley's oldest son and daughter-in-law. I made arrangements with the funeral home. I told them I wanted a simple graveside service where my mother would rest next to my father.

"What type of rabbi-Orthodox, Conservative or Reformed?" the funeral director asked.

"It has to be Orthodox; my grandfather was an Orthodox rabbi," I proudly said.

Rabbi Shusterman called me later at Shirley's son's home. I told him who my grandfather was.

"I've read his books," he said.

He asked me my mother's Hebrew name and to tell him things about her so he could write the eulogy.

"Her Hebrew name is Shayna Yetta, but I'll deliver the eulogy, Rabbi," I said.

That evening, as Shirley's son and daughter-in-law slept, I stayed awake, alone, and sat on the windowsill in their living room with paper and pencil, thinking about what to say. I thought of Wicker Park so many, many years ago. I remembered that my mother had always worn an apron when we had no company. I remembered that she always gave me two Twinkies for lunch and that she was always working or dusting while listening to her radio programs. Her dresses were all short sleeved. She wore black laced shoes. And whenever I was too quiet playing alone, she would always holler out,

"Sherwin," or walk back to my room to make sure I was there.

I remembered how Uncle Sam would push his foot on our car's floor starter button ...putt, putt, putt. He would push again and again, and my mother would holler, "Sam, you don't know what you're doing." And then one more push and the motor would run. I loved standing on the running board waiting for us to get going. And that tall chrome-plated hood ornament with the body of a winged dragon and the claws of an eagle -it was fascinating. All eight of us would pile into the four-door blue car, with me sitting on my mother's lap, for our Sunday ride and trip to Navy Pier, with its Ferris wheel and other rides, picnic tables, and boat rides on Lake Michigan.

"Slow down, slow down Sam, ...you drive too fast," my mother would holler nastily. Then Ojeh would pick up my mother's lead. "Sam, Sam, slow down."

Onnie would crumple. "Sam, Sam."

My father, Deanie, Shirley and I would just enjoy the ride. And when I had my tonsils and adenoids taken out and was back at home, my mother would come to my room and feed me ice cream as I knelt in my crib. As she left, she would pull the guard rail back up... Hell, I was five years old.

And the instructions she gave to Shirley when I started kindergarten: "Don't let him out of your sight when you walk to school." She would say the same thing every day.

My mother would never let me cross the street to Wicker Park alone. God forbid a car should come along that short, all but deserted street. I remember walking to Milwaukee Avenue to go shopping, and my mother stopping to talk to friends and acquaintances.

"Your boy's so cute," they'd all say. "And such beautiful black curly hair."

I hated it when my mother agreed about my pretty curly hair. I would pull on her dress. "Ma, let's go...Ma, let's go."

"Just a minute. Just a minute, Sherwin," she would always say.

Even then, I had a sense of timing, "Ma, Ma, it's a minute, let's go," I would exclaim as I tugged harder on her dress.

But she always let me play in the alley with the neighborhood kids. As I would walk down the winding wooden staircase at the back of the third floor, she would always call out, "Hold on to the railing going down."

And when I got scratches, she would paint them with Mercurochrome and if it was serious, I would suffer through iodine. I can remember her giving me brown laxatives that looked and chewed like candy although they didn't taste very good...and if my illness was really serious, I would get an enema. She would apply Vaseline to my asshole and then stick that black nozzle up my ass and let the hot water flush me out. I would always cry when I got my enema but I will admit those results were immediate as I ran naked to the toilet, making it just in time. And then she'd finish off her doctoring with a tablespoon of milk of magnesia, the wonder drug of that day.

And then one day the car was gone...later the horse and wagon were gone. I would see my father push his empty pushcart to the side of the alley under the elevated tracks, come up the back staircase and eat what my mother had prepared. And after my father had gone to Louisville and gotten a job, he wrote for us to come. We could have gone free by truck. The place where he worked would have an empty truck going from Chicago back to Louisville. It would take some of the furniture we had, and my mother and me too. But my mother said, "Or we can take the train; it's up to you.

One half of my friends said, "Take the truck. It's fun." The other half said, "Take the train. It's fun." It was my decision to make. The first big decision of my life and I was not yet six and a half.

"Ma, let's take the train," I said. And that was the last time my mother was ever overprotective of me.

I remembered all about Louisville and all the other times I'd spent with my mother. I remembered how my mother had never liked Sam. I couldn't understand it. I not only liked my Uncle Sam, I loved my Uncle Sam. As my thoughts faded, I softly said aloud the words I had never said while my mother was alive. "Ma...I love you!" And then I picked up the pencil and paper and wrote.

At the funeral home I joined my cousin Shirley and my father's youngest brother's wife, my Aunt Dora. The three of us followed the hearse in our limousine, and behind us, Rabbi Shusterman drove alone in his car.

As we parked near the cemetery plot, I saw many other cars there. I nodded my thanks to all the relatives and almost-relatives who had come. I stood next to the rabbi to give the eulogy before the casket was lowered. On the other side of the open grave, standing closest to me, with tears in her eyes, was my cousin Shirley. I pulled from my jacket the paper I'd scribbled on the night before and read:

Shayna Yetta, may the messenger of God guide your soul safely through the inner worlds...and may you once again experience and become a part of the essence of those you loved so dearly:

Your father, Rabbi Saul Shochet; your mother, Faige Dinah Shochet; your daughter, Fay Ernst; your husband, Morris Ernst; your brother, Morris Shochet, your sister, Jennie Finkelstein; your niece, Ethel Finkelstein; and your niece, Deanie Chaskin.

May you enjoy the blessings of heaven for all eternity, and may God accept you for all eternity... And never shall you return to this world of human suffering.

Amen.

End

Epilogue

Years after my experience with Yogananda, Sandy and I were initiated by Kirpal Singh's successor, Sant Darshan Singh Ji Maharaj.

My contract with the insurance company was bought out and the stars were no longer with me on other business ventures I pursued.

I saw Sarah again in California on two separate occasions. I still keep in touch with Sylvia and Shirley.

Matthew is a stockbroker. Lynda works in a real estate office. Jon writes songs, sings and plays the piano. Sandy is a successful real estate broker and now has red hair. And me? Well...I wrote a book.

Me and my cousin Shirley on our back porch in Wicker Park,
c. 1935

Riding my favorite Schwinn bike around Chicago,
c. 1942

Me outside our apartment on Walnut street in Louisville,
c. 1945

Hanging out in Chicago with nieces Fay and Bobbi,
c. 1950

Flying solo in Wichita Falls, TX c. 1951

Man about town in Paris, France c. 1953

My parents, Morris and Ethel, in Chicago, c.1953

My biological mother Sarah, c. 1961

Sandy and me at our wedding reception, November 18, 1961

*Sandy and me signing in after hours at the LaSalle Street office
(pregnant with Matthew) c. 1963*

Me with sister Sylvia, meeting for the first time in Canoga Park, c. August 1963

The five of us together in Chicago, c. 1972

Picture of spirits in the living room window of our Montrose Avenue apartment, captured by my Rolleiflex camera, c. 1964

Artist rendering of above "spirit picture" taken at our Montrose apartment

Me channelling The Zadik in Chicago, c. 1978

Made in the USA
Las Vegas, NV
13 July 2023

74683342R00134